PEOPLE
IN THE NEWS

Orlando Bloom

Titles in the People in the News series include:

PEOPLE
IN THE NEWS

Orlando Bloom

by Terri Dougherty

LUCENT BOOKS
A part of Gale, Cengage Learning

GALE
CENGAGE Learning™

Detroit • New York • San Francisco • New Haven, Conn • Waterville, Maine • London

© 2006 Gale, a part of Cengage Learning

For more information, contact
Lucent Books
27500 Drake Rd.
Farmington Hills, MI 48331-3535
Or you can visit our Internet site at gale.cengage.com

LIBRARY OF CONGRESS CATALOGING-IN-PUBLICATION DATA

Dougherty, Terri.
  Orlando Bloom / by Terri Dougherty.
    p. cm. — (People in the news)
  Includes bibliographical references and index.
  ISBN 1-59018-714-8 (hard cover : alk. paper)
  1. Bloom, Orlando, 1977– —Juvenile literature. 2. Motion picture actors and actresses—Great Britain—Biography—Juvenile literature. I. Title. II. Series: People in the news (San Diego, Calif.)
  PN2598.B6394D68 2005
  791.4302'8'092—dc22

                                                                    2005012878

Printed in the United States of America
5 6 7 12 11 10 09 08

Table of Contents

Foreword

FAME AND CELEBRITY are alluring. People are drawn to those who walk in fame's spotlight, whether they are known for great accomplishments or for notorious deeds. The lives of the famous pique public interest and attract attention, perhaps because their experiences seem in some ways so different from, yet in other ways so similar to, our own.

Newspapers, magazines, and television regularly capitalize on this fascination with celebrity by running profiles of famous people. For example, television programs such as *Entertainment Tonight* devote all of their programming to stories about entertainment and entertainers. Magazines such as *People* fill their pages with stories of the private lives of famous people. Even newspapers, newsmagazines, and television news frequently delve into the lives of well-known personalities. Despite the number of articles and programs, few provide more than a superficial glimpse at their subjects.

Lucent's People in the News series offers young readers a deeper look into the lives of today's news makers, the influences that have shaped them, and the impact they have had in their fields of endeavor and on other people's lives. The subjects of the series hail from many disciplines and walks of life. They include authors, musicians, athletes, political leaders, entertainers, entrepreneurs, and others who have made a mark on modern life and who, in many cases, will continue to do so for years to come.

These biographies are more than factual chronicles. Each book emphasizes the contributions, accomplishments, or deeds that have brought fame or notoriety to the individual and shows how that person has influenced modern life. Authors portray their subjects in a realistic, unsentimental light. For example, Bill Gates—the cofounder and chief executive officer of the software giant Microsoft—has been instrumental in making personal computers the most vital tool of the modern age. Few dispute his business savvy, his perseverance, or his technical expertise, yet critics say he is ruthless in his dealings with competitors and driven more by his desire to maintain Microsoft's dominance in the computer industry than by an interest in furthering technology.

In these books, young readers will encounter inspiring stories about real people who achieved success despite enormous obstacles. Oprah Winfrey—the most powerful, most watched, and wealthiest woman on television today—spent the first six years of her life in the care of her grandparents while her unwed mother sought work and a better life elsewhere. Her adolescence was colored by promiscuity, pregnancy at age fourteen, rape, and sexual abuse.

Each author documents and supports his or her work with an array of primary and secondary source quotations taken from diaries, letters, speeches, and interviews. All quotes are footnoted to show readers exactly how and where biographers derive their information and provide guidance for further research. The quotations enliven the text by giving readers eyewitness views of the life and accomplishments of each person covered in the People in the News series.

In addition, each book in the series includes photographs, annotated bibliographies, timelines, and comprehensive indexes. For both the casual reader and the student researcher, the People in the News series offers insight into the lives of today's news makers—people who shape the way we live, work, and play in the modern age.

Introduction

Orlando's Magic

From a casual glance at his career, it seems Orlando Bloom has glided effortlessly to stardom. He won a part in the blockbuster *The Lord of the Rings* right after leaving drama school at age twenty-two and nabbed a role in *Pirates of the Caribbean* with veteran actor Johnny Depp a few years later. He continued to make a name for himself, in sweeping historical dramas, as he acted with Brad Pitt in *Troy* and took the lead in Ridley Scott's *Kingdom of Heaven*. As acting careers go, his has begun on a scale of epic proportions.

The word "challenge" does not seem to be appropriate when discussing such a career, yet that is precisely the word that keeps cropping up when Bloom's life is examined. As a boy and teen, Bloom approached life exuberantly and loved to challenge himself to take chances. However, this enthusiasm led to many accidents and almost cost him his life. While he showed talent for acting at a young age, he had to first learn that there were consequences to his sometimes ill-thought-out decisions if he was going to have an opportunity to use his ability to act.

From a young age Bloom adored performing, but never set his sights on becoming a star. As he watched actors onstage and in movies, he admired how they went about portraying their characters without paying much attention to the fame that could come along with their work. He wanted to be an actor, but not necessarily a star. However, fame came his way soon after he appeared as the blond elf Legolas in *The Lord of the Rings* movie trilogy. Sudden stardom and a new status as a teen heartthrob became another challenge for Bloom, as he

Since taking the movie world by storm with his role as Legolas in the blockbuster The Lord of the Rings *trilogy, Orlando Bloom has become one of Hollywood's most sought-after stars.*

now had to manage a career that he had not expected to flourish so quickly.

Since bursting onto the movie scene in *The Lord of the Rings*, Bloom has become a Hollywood heartthrob. As a classically trained actor, Bloom never expected to get more attention for his looks than for the roles he played. While he does not deny that his handsome features are part of the reason for his popularity and that his good looks help him get considered for movie roles, he does not want to star in pictures that showcase only his looks. He wants audiences to enjoy watching the characters he embodies.

Bloom considers himself fortunate to have been tapped for roles in big-budget productions and has made a conscious effort to learn every time he steps in front of the camera. Few people have heard of *The Calcium Kid* or *Haven*, yet Bloom considers these smaller pictures as low-pressure opportunities for him to become a better actor. These character-driven movies, which have not received critical acclaim or widespread release, allow him to flex his acting muscles and put to use the skills he learned in drama school.

In his first major movies Bloom was happy to get secondary parts, which took the pressure off him to make the movie succeed. In addition, he could learn from the actors he was working with. Those roles prepared him to take on the lead in films such as *Kingdom of Heaven* and *Elizabethtown*, which allowed him to challenge himself to take risks with his career and test his ability to become a leading man.

While Bloom appears to have easily made the transition from drama student to star, he has put much thought into how to guide his career. He has capitalized on his fame with roles in big-budget productions, but has not embraced his pretty boy image. Keeping a low profile, he tries to keep his personal life quiet while choosing interesting and diverse roles that will lay the foundation for a long acting career. Always looking to improve as an actor, Bloom likes to challenge himself with each new role and each career step.

Chapter 1

Untamed Enthusiasm

ORLANDO BLOOM WAS born on January 13, 1977, in Canterbury, England, a city about 60 miles (96.56 km) southeast of London. His mother, Sonia Copeland-Bloom, ran a language school for foreign students. She was married to Harry Bloom, a professor of law at the University of Kent in Canterbury.

Harry Bloom often had trouble remembering the names of students in his class, so Orlando's mother gave her son a memorable name. She named him after Orlando Gibbons, a seventeenth-century composer and organist, and his family called him "Orli" for short. Orlando has a sister, Samantha, who is two years older than he.

Orlando was born into a worldly family. Harry Bloom, who was sixty-four when Orlando was born, was a writer and law professor. He had lived in South Africa, and as a lawyer had championed the rights of blacks there at a time when the country's apartheid policies supported segregation and discrimination. Harry Bloom's most famous book was *Transvaal Episode*, a novel about an uprising in a South African town. The book, published in 1956, was banned by the South African government because of fears it would lead to increased racial tensions in the country. However, it was sold around the world, and opened people's eyes to the racial inequities in South Africa.

Bloom worked with others who were active in the anti-apartheid movement, including political activist Nelson Mandela, who would one day become South Africa's president. In the early 1960s Bloom spent three months in prison for standing up for his antiapartheid beliefs. He left South Africa in 1963 to take a post as professor of law at the University of Kent.

Orlando's mother named her son after Orlando Gibbons, a seventeenth-century English composer and organist.

In Kent, Bloom met Sonia Copeland. She was a writer, businesswoman, and founder of the Concorde International school. The school in Canterbury gave foreign students the opportunity to learn English and sharpen their language skills. Orlando describes his mother as an adventurous woman, who was not afraid to try new things and do what she wanted with her life. She taught him that nothing was impossible, and that taking risks was an important part of life.

Sonia Copeland-Bloom had the greater parental influence on Orlando's childhood, as Harry Bloom died in 1981 at the age of sixty-eight. Orlando, who was four at the time, was too young to have amassed firm memories of the activist writer and legal scholar. However, as he grew up, Orlando learned of Bloom's accomplishments and came to admire him and his work. He wished he could have known him better. "Harry was always a role model for me," Orlando says as an adult. "My mother spoke of him so fondly."[1]

Aches and Pains

As a young child, Orlando had to adjust to life without a father. His mother helped him make it through this emotionally painful experience, but the loss of his father was not the only pain Orlando would experience as a youngster. Orlando also had to deal with some physically painful situations, as from a very young age he was prone to getting hurt.

These accidents began when Orlando was a few months old. His mother was carrying him while gathering wood, and she accidentally knocked his head against a tree when she bent over. A few months later, he again injured his skull when he fell off a kitchen stool. As a young boy he was introduced to horses, and was injured when one stepped on his foot and crushed a toe.

Orlando was an energetic youngster who had a tendency to jump before he realized how hard the landing would be. His reckless nature led to a number of bruises and broken bones. He took so many trips to the hospital as a youngster, he said, that the staff worried he was being beaten. That was not the case; it was instead Orlando's propensity for running headfirst into action that caused his body to take a beating.

Challenges at School

Orlando loved to play action-oriented games of pretend, and he had a vivid imagination that helped him get along with other children and enjoy his childhood. He liked playing pirates and pretending to be Superman, and loved taking on the characteristics of different people. "Orlando was a very normal boy, full of action, full of ideas, totally and absolutely normal,"[2] says Copeland-Bloom.

This is an aerial view of Canterbury, the English city in Kent where Orlando was born and raised.

Orlando got along well with other children, but always had one initial obstacle to overcome. When he met people for the first time, he always had to convince them that his name really was Orlando. While his name was memorable, it also set him apart from the other children his age, and he sometimes felt it was difficult to live up to a name that was so special.

Orlando went to school at St. Edmund's, an expensive private coed institution in Canterbury. His mother had to sacrifice to help her son with his education, but the investment turned out to have been a wise one. Orlando is mildly dyslexic, and the learning disability made it difficult for him to learn to read. At the private school he could get the extra attention he needed. Academic subjects were not easy for Orlando, and it was hard for him to complete his assignments. While he received help from his teachers and his mother in dealing with his dyslexia, his difficulties did not pass by unnoticed by other students, and he was sometimes teased because he was a slow reader and poor speller. Generally a well-liked student, however, Orlando persevered with his schoolwork. His talent for drama helped, as his teachers took note of his ability in performance. He also did well in art classes, especially with ceramics and sculpture. He eventually overcame his reading difficulty well enough to do the script reading he needed to do as an actor.

Enchanted by Actors

Despite the problems he had with his schoolwork, Orlando had a happy childhood. His imagination always offered him a place to escape to when homework weighed him down. School plays and performing also interested him, although his first appearance onstage was not pleasant.

At age four, Orlando played a monkey in a play at a local theater in Canterbury. It seemed to him that the whole city was there, watching him onstage as one of three monkeys. He was dressed in a synthetic suit, and his costume was hot and itchy. When his behind began to itch, he scratched it, thinking it was something that a monkey would do. The audience thought his action was hilarious, and broke out in laughter. Orlando had not

Super Dreams

When Orlando was in grade school a game he played with his class-
mates helped pique his interest in acting. "There was a girl in my class
whom all the guys had a crush on," he recalled in *The Lord of the Rings
Official Movie Guide* by Brian Sibley. "We used to run races in the play-
ground at lunchtime to see who would be her boyfriend for the day!
I had always loved watching *Superman* on television, and I used to
fantasize that I could just fly in, pick up the girl and zoom off again!"
While he realized that Superman was being played by an actor, he
began to think that acting like Superman or another character would
be a great job to have.

meant to do anything funny and was embarrassed. However, he
did not let the incident inhibit his desire for acting. "I did a lot
of plays at school, and I was always encouraged," Orlando says.
"I found theater a very comfortable place. I was good at learning lines, and I had the confidence to get up there and deliver
them. I took it quite seriously."[3]

Copeland-Bloom encouraged Orlando and his sister to
develop an appreciation for the theater and a love for acting and
the arts. She took them to the Marlowe Theatre in Canterbury,
and with her the children would also stop and watch street per-
formers who entertained crowds in the city. She emphasized the
visual arts as well, and had Samantha and Orlando take art and
pottery lessons from teachers who came to their home.

Orlando's mother also encouraged him and Samantha to go
onstage themselves, and they competed in Bible and poetry
reading contests. The contests made a lasting impression on
Orlando, and years later he could still recite the lines from
Robert Frost's poem "Stopping by Woods on a Snowy Evening,"
which he had memorized as a young boy. The positive feedback
he received from his experiences with the recitation contests fed
his desire to act. "That's where I got a real taste for performing,"
Orlando recalls. "I'd love to stand up and perform, and I'd do
quite well."[4]

In addition to doing recitations, acting was another natural
outlet for Orlando's interest in performing. From a young age he
used to think about what it would be like to be acting onstage or

One of Orlando's first onstage performances as a young boy, was a recitation of a poem by Robert Frost (pictured).

in a television show. It would be a place where he could put his imagination and creativity to use. He became even more interested in it when he saw how actors could take on different personalities and could become new people with each role. "When I realized that the heroes on 'The A-Team' and 'The Fall Guy' and 'Knight Rider' weren't real, I decided I wanted to act, because I thought 'I'd love to be any number of those guys,'"[5] he says.

Orlando's teachers recognized his ability and he was given interesting roles in school plays. He was proud of his turn as the sergeant of police in Gilbert and Sullivan's operetta *The Pirates of Penzance*, which he performed at St. Edmund's. He also played an old man in the musical *The Boy Friend* at the school. While he was not often given the lead in school productions, he was given roles that let him bring personality to a character and presented opportunities to experiment and enjoy what he was doing.

Bad Breaks

Orlando's acting experiences in grade school were temporarily curtailed by his penchant for broken bones. He was not afraid to push himself into risky situations, and his body paid the price. When he was eleven, Orlando broke his leg in a skiing accident. His leg was put into a cast, and it took a year to heal properly.

Orlando's broken leg curtailed his activity, and because he could not get out and run around with his friends he gained weight. It was a difficult time for the normally energetic and active youngster, and he could not help feeling sorry for himself. "I sat at home really depressed because I couldn't play. I was eating biscuits [cookies] and chocolate bars," he says. "I was a porker."[6]

After the cast came off, Orlando resumed his adventurous activities. Despite having recently recovered from a broken leg, he did not hold back in friendly competition. When he was twelve, he broke his nose and a finger while playing rugby.

These injuries did not make him more cautious, however. He continued to crave adventure and the pursuit of new activities, and at age thirteen tried snowboarding for the first time. He

His Own Style

Acting roles were not the only way Orlando chose to express himself. He was intent on creating his own individual sense of style. As a teen, he had some help from his older sister and one of his best friends in this endeavor. He and his friend used to wear vintage 1960s clothing they found stored at his friend's home, and his sister added to Orlando's unique look by buying clothing for him from secondhand shops. Orlando wanted to make an impression on people who saw him, both onstage and off.

took on a hill that was too difficult for a beginner, and broke a wrist. Orlando was a child who loved to play as hard as he could, and did not always think about what could happen to him because of his actions. "I was a little bit crazy," he says. "Not crazy-crazy, but I was always the first one to jump off the wall or dive into the lake, without really thinking about the consequences."[7]

Family Secret

Orlando weathered his broken bones and the physical aches and pains of his childhood, but at age thirteen was confronted with a different kind of jolt. He had always thought of Harry Bloom as his father. However, when the young teen was on vacation with his family, his mother revealed some startling information to him and his sister.

Copeland-Bloom told Orlando and Samantha that Harry Bloom was not their biological father. Their father was Colin Stone, a family friend. Orlando had gotten to know Stone because the man had helped care for Harry Bloom after Bloom suffered a stroke. After Harry Bloom died, Stone became the guardian of Orlando and Samantha.

Orlando was surprised by the news, but not bitter, broken-hearted, or hurt. He came to understand how difficult it must have been for his mother to tell her children this, and he regards his paternity as a bit of family history that makes him a little more interesting. He still looks upon Harry Bloom as his father, and Stone as a good friend.

The news did not alter Orlando's good-humored nature; he was happy as a child and he grew up in a loving family. Years later, Orlando commented philosophically to a reporter that most families had a few skeletons in the closet, and his was no different. "My mom was married to one man, but I was fathered by a second," he explains. "I think she was waiting for me to be old enough to understand it. But when would you tell a kid about that stuff? It's very difficult."[8]

Expressing Himself

Throughout a childhood marked by multiple broken bones and one uncomfortable revelation, Orlando maintained an exuberance for life. He played hard when he was with his friends, and continued to express himself through plays at school. His acting talent was evident, and when it came time to try out for the roles in plays, he would win the lead against students who were several years older than he was. He was also known as a good-looking student, but he impressed his drama teacher with his acting ability. "I think it's easy to forget that Orlando was an excellent actor," says Richard Parsons, his drama teacher at St. Edmund's. "Even at 14 or 15 he was getting lead roles against people who were 17 or 18."[9]

Movies and television interested Orlando, as he remained fascinated by the way an actor could lose himself in a role. When he was around age twelve, Orlando and his family visited relatives in Boston, and a cousin who was an art director in Los Angeles rented some movies for the group to watch. One of them was the 1961 movie *The Hustler,* starring Paul Newman, which Orlando at first thought would be dull because it was in black and white. Instead, Orlando was enthralled by the way Newman coolly portrayed his character. In addition, Orlando was impressed when he saw movies starring James Dean, the actor who starred in the 1955 film *Rebel Without a Cause* and was killed in a car accident that same year. The passion Dean showed in his work made an impression on young Orlando. Other early influences on Orlando's career choice included Daniel Day-Lewis, with his role in *The Last of the Mohicans.*

James Dean appears in a movie still from his most famous film, Rebel Without a Cause. *Dean's passionate acting inspired the young Orlando.*

An Actor's Life

As a teen, Orlando was finding himself drawn more and more toward acting and the theater, not only as a childhood diversion but as a possible career. His mother continued to encourage his interest in the arts by taking him to plays, and he participated in community theater projects. Schoolwork was not easy for Orlando and, although he continued to do his best, his heart was leading him away from academics.

Orlando passed his school examinations, earning his highest grades in theater, art, and sculpture. The arts were clearly his strength. He was impressed by what he had seen other actors do, and for his own acting had consistently received compliments. His mother, who had taken him to the theater and introduced him to Shakespeare, encouraged him to pursue his dream. Acting seemed to hold the most promise for his future.

While schoolwork had not been Orlando's strength, he was not taking the easy way out by pursuing acting. He got scared and nervous whenever he stepped onstage, and one of the things that drew him to performing was the challenge of appearing before an audience. Working at overcoming that fear and the feeling of accomplishment that came from facing his fear head-on kept him going back for more.

Acting also allowed the thrill-seeking Orlando to bring more adventure into his life. At age sixteen he left home to continue his education in London. Instead of going on to more traditional schooling, Orlando prepared to study at Britain's National Youth Theatre.

Chapter 2

Life-Changing Experience

ORLANDO WAS AN adventurous teen who knew what he wanted from life. By his midteens he had made acting his career choice, and had left Canterbury to study acting in London. He felt that moving to the city and studying there would give him his best chance of launching a career as an actor. London was home to numerous theaters and a thriving arts scene, and if Orlando's talent was to be noticed by someone, he knew he had to put himself in the middle of the action. Here he would be able to find out if the talent he had shown in school productions in Canterbury could be honed into a professional career.

London also appealed to Orlando's thirst for excitement. The city offered plenty of social opportunities, and the crowds and clubs instantly caught his attention. Although still a teen, he was drawn to the social atmosphere of an older crowd. The fearless nature he had shown as a child would continue to be evident during the latter half of his teen years.

City Life

When Orlando first arrived in London, the city was a lonely place for him. He had left his circle of friends in Canterbury and did not make new friends as quickly as he had expected. It was not until he settled into an apartment in the Camden district of London that he began meeting people and enjoying the entertainment the city had to offer.

After making friends, Orlando enthusiastically began exploring the city with them. He became friends with an older group of students, and quickly added visiting the city's nightclubs to his list of adventurous things to do. "That was a big growth period for me," Orlando says. "Me and my friends, who were mostly older, used to go clubbing, and I experienced a lot of life at a young age because of that."[10] While Orlando had a good time with his friends, he did not neglect his commitment to the theater. In addition to attending theater classes, he also studied sculpture and photography.

Orlando spent two seasons with the youth theater. While there he got his first job as an actor, in an episode of the British television drama series *Casualty* in 1994. He played a self-mutilator, a person who cuts himself for attention. It was a dark, somber role for the young actor, but he appreciated the experience it gave him.

Drawn to London's numerous theaters, the teenage Orlando moved to the capital city to study acting.

Bloom's Artistic Side

If Bloom had not become interested in acting, he might have become a sculptor. His mother encouraged him to be interested in many aspects of the arts, and one of his teachers noted that he was talented in making ceramic projects. In school, he got better grades on his sculpture exam than he did on his exam for theater studies.

"My mum is always going, 'Just keep up the sculpture, darling,'—she's convinced she's gonna have a little shop somewhere and sell my sculptures someday," he told an *Entertainment Weekly* interviewer for its 2003 IT List.

Drama Academy

After Orlando's second season with the youth theater, he was offered a scholarship to another acting institution, the British American Drama Academy. While there he won the lead in the play *Tales from the Vienna Woods*. The play, set in 1930 in Vienna, was written by Odon von Horvath; it tells the unhappy story of an engaged woman who leaves her fiancé for another man and suffers for making the wrong choices. It was a serious play, and Orlando's success in landing that role and others confirmed to him that he was on the right track with his life. He took it as a compliment every time he was offered a part.

Orlando had moved to London in order to put himself into a setting where he could come into contact with influential people in the acting arena, and his plan paid off during his appearance in *Tales from the Vienna Woods* at the Tricycle Theatre in North London. His work impressed an agent who saw him in the play, and led to his signing with a talent agency. The agency would now be there to help him have more opportunities to audition for more plays and bigger roles.

Wilde

In 1997, Orlando landed his first part in a movie. The film was *Wilde*, a biographical movie about the life of controversial Irish playwright Oscar Wilde. The movie starred Stephen Fry and included Jude Law and Vanessa Redgrave in the cast. Bloom had a small role—only one line—but the 1997 film received good reviews and allowed Bloom to continue to gain exposure as an actor.

Bloom's career was moving forward at a slow, yet steady pace. He was far from being well known, but was consistently getting roles and had won parts on television, the stage, and screen. Although his career was still in its infancy, Bloom had achieved his goal of becoming an actor.

However, although he was getting work, Bloom did not feel the roles he was getting were helping him learn enough about his craft. In order to grow as an actor, he wanted to learn more about the writers who created the roles he was portraying, as well as improve his acting skills. In order to do this, he decided to return to school. He felt that continuing his education, rather than continuing to audition for small parts in the theater, television, and movies, would help him advance his career.

Back to School

Bloom was a good actor, but knew he could become a better one. To do this, in 1997 he enrolled in a three-year program at the Guildhall School of Music and Drama in London. The school had a solid reputation, and actors Ewan McGregor and Joseph Fiennes had trained there. Bloom would walk past their pictures on his way to class, their faces reminding him and other students that it was possible to achieve success in acting by using the school as a launching pad.

Bloom's goal was to become an actor on the stage, and the prestigious London academy was a place where he could learn in the company of other actors. "I always planned to go to drama school," he says. "I suppose I could have trained in the industry more. But, instead, I chose an environment that would be more conducive to experimenting."[11]

At Guildhall, Bloom had more artistic freedom than he would have had if he had continued to train by going to auditions. Whereas in a professional environment he was expected to know what he was doing, at the school Bloom could take chances, make mistakes, and learn from them. He would be able to participate in a number of plays, representing varied theatrical styles.

Classical Training

Some of Bloom's first onstage experiences at the school came in classical dramas such as *Antigone*, a tragedy written in 442 B.C. by Sophocles. Bloom also had a role in *The Trojan Women*, written by Euripides in 415 B.C. In *The Trojan Women*, he played Menelaus, the husband of Helen of Troy, the woman whose abduction sparks the Trojan War. Bloom's familiarity with these Greek classics would become beneficial after he became a professional actor, when he would play Paris, the man who takes Helen from her husband, in the movie *Troy*.

At Guildhall, Bloom had the opportunity to hone his acting talent in a variety of roles. He appeared in both classics and

In 1997 Orlando made his film debut with a small part in Wilde, *a movie about the life of Irish playwright Oscar Wilde.*

modern theater offerings. He played a military officer in *The Recruiting Officer*, a drama set in the early 1700s, and had a role as a bully in the 1960s play *A Night Out*. He also appeared in an adaptation of traditional mystery plays, medieval representations of biblical events. His dramatic experience at Guildhall continued with roles in *Twelfth Night* by William Shakespeare, *Uncle Vanya* by Anton Chekhov, and a singing role in the musical *Little Me*.

These plays were giving Bloom solid grounding in classic theater. He was learning how to embrace a role that had been tried on by many generations of actors before him, and make it his own. Bloom had the opportunity to appear in small television roles while he was at Guildhall, but turned most of them down to concentrate on his stage work. In 1998 he appeared in the television sketch show *Smack the Pony*, but spent the majority of his time concentrating his acting efforts onstage.

Frightening Accident

Bloom's acting career was moving along at a satisfying pace. The work at school was intense, with many plays to read, lines to memorize, and authors to learn about, but Bloom was getting the classical grounding in theater he had been looking for. He was challenging himself as an actor and enjoying his studies. His adventurous spirit, however, was not confined to the stage. It

Odd Jobs

While he was in drama school, Orlando worked at part-time jobs to earn extra money. He worked at clothing stores such as Paul Smith and Boxfresh in London as a way to earn cash and support his clothing habit.

He liked working in the clothing shops better than the job he had had when he was younger. He had been a clay pigeon trapper, working at a shooting range. He pulled the trap lever that made the clay disks fly into the air, so the marksmen could practice their aim by shooting at them. He later called it the worst job he ever had. "I always wanted to be the shooter," he said as quoted in *Entertainment Weekly*'s 2003 IT List.

would almost cost him dearly as his unwillingness to turn down a challenge would result in a serious injury.

His career, and his life, almost came to an end during his second year at the school. On a Sunday afternoon in 1998, the twenty-one-year-old was hanging around with some friends at their apartment. The group decided to head up to the roof terrace, but the door to the terrace would not budge. They could not open it by trying to force it from the inside, and determined that it would have to be kicked in from the outside. Always ready for an adventure, Bloom volunteered to climb out the window and up to the roof in order to open the door.

Bloom thought he could make it to a roof terrace landing that was one level down, and then climb up to the roof of the apartment. Without looking down, he climbed out the window, intending to jump to the landing below him. However, he missed the landing and had to grab on to a drainpipe. The drainpipe could not support his weight and came loose. Bloom fell three stories. He broke his back and several ribs, and was rushed to the hospital.

Denial

Bloom had broken many bones before but had never gone through anything like this. He crushed one vertebra and fractured three others. Doctors had sobering news for him. They told Bloom he would never walk again.

Used to being independent and self-assured, Bloom hated being an invalid. Nurses had to wash him, move him, and do everything for him. He could only lie on his back and think about what had happened to him. "I feel like it really tested my belief in myself and everything else because they told me I'd be in a wheelchair," Bloom says. "It took a while for me to really comprehend what had happened."[12]

Bloom was shocked by the severity of his injuries. He did not want to believe what the doctors were telling him. He had taken risks and had been injured before, but never so badly. It felt to him as if the doctors were talking to someone else. "I was really depressed," he recalls. "I was in a lot of pain. But I had

Bloom's recovery from a near-fatal accident caused the young actor to adopt a more mature view of life.

this one great teacher who came to visit and said to me, 'This is going to be the making of you.' And it was."[13]

Recovery

Bloom struggled mentally as well as physically as he tried to comprehend what had happened. For four days, it looked as if he would never walk again. Then his doctors decided that he could undergo an operation that would give him a chance at regaining the use of his legs. Doctors were doubtful of its chances for success, and Bloom ran the risk of having severe damage to his bones and nerves, but he took the chance. Always one to take risks, he could not imagine living life without being able to be active and do things as he had always done. He wanted at least to try to have the opportunity to walk again.

The operation was a success. Twelve days later, Bloom hobbled out of the hospital, moving with the aid of crutches. He would be able to walk again, but needed to learn how to do it.

For a year, Bloom had to wear a brace. He went through intensive rehabilitation and gradually learned to walk. During physical therapy, he practiced walking by telling himself how to do it. He would repeat "heel, ball, toe" on every step he took as he painstakingly taught himself to walk again. The accident tested his resolve, and changed the way he looked at life.

New Attitude

His near-fatal fall made Bloom reflect on the way he was living. He was determined to face the physical challenges the accident brought; as he did so, he became aware of all that he had taken for granted. Bloom had always embraced and enjoyed life, but he now appreciated things much more and saw every day as an opportunity. He realized that he was lucky to walk, and, indeed, lucky to be alive. "It's really made me appreciate life more because everything now is a bit of a bonus," he said a few years later. "I still get the odd twang every now and again, but having a little pain in my back reminds me how lucky I am. It also focused me—and refocused me—to make everything more real."[14]

Part of Bloom's training at Guildhall included studying the classics of William Shakespeare and other timeless playwrights.

The accident made Bloom take a more mature approach toward his actions. During his youth, Bloom had courted danger without thinking about potential negative consequences. He could not wait to be the first to climb a tree so he could fall out of it. He assumed everything would turn out fine. But that attitude had almost cost Bloom his life and had almost taken away his dream of becoming an actor. He was not going to make that mistake again.

Bloom now realized that there was more to life than a series of exciting but irresponsible or dangerous actions. He needed to slow down and think about what he was doing. "I was running around like a little lunatic, not really appreciating life or the people around me," he says. "I didn't address the consequences. I would jump ledges, and I never thought about what was on the other side. I just assumed there would be a soft landing."[15]

Back to the Stage

Bloom gradually recovered and was strong enough to return to the stage in the fall of 1998. He had a small role in *Mephisto*, by the great twentieth-century German writer Thomas Mann, at Guildhall that November. He also appeared in *Peer Gynt*, by Norwegian playwright Henrik Ibsen, in February 1999. As part of his work at Guildhall, he was also studying classics by Milton, Chekhov, and Shakespeare, learning from the authors whose work had endured for centuries. From them, he was gaining insight into the complexities of the human spirit so he would be better equipped to bring a wide array of emotions alive on stage.

During 1999 there was also excitement in the air as the students learned about a casting process for a major movie series. Although students were discouraged from auditioning for professional roles while at the school, Bloom's agent kept his name in front of casting directors. When he heard that director Peter Jackson was conducting a worldwide search for actors to appear in his cinematic adaptation of J.R.R. Tolkien's *The Lord of the Rings*, Bloom was thrilled to be able to make an audition tape.

Graduating with Honors

The casting process for *The Lord of the Rings* was immense, and Jackson auditioned hundreds of actors for the fifteen major roles in the film. Agents from Los Angeles to London were notified that a search was being conducted for actors to take on roles in the major project, and they called their clients to encourage them to audition. Many of the other aspiring actors Bloom knew were also up for roles in *Rings*. It seemed to him that everyone was drawn to the epic tale of nine friends on a quest to save the world from evil.

When Bloom made an audition tape for the movie, it was for the role of Faramir, one of two brothers from the ruling family in a kingdom threatened by the evil Sauron. Bloom would have been thrilled to get the role, although it was a minor one. When six months passed without any word Bloom thought he had little chance of getting the part.

He did not have much time to worry about it, however, as he was busy with classes and plays at Guildhall. He later said that he was happy that he had been too busy to think about actually cap-

Bad-Boy Performance

Before taking on the role of Legolas, Bloom had one more commitment to fulfill. The day after being told he had been chosen for *The Lord of the Rings*, he learned that he had been selected for a role in the British television drama *Midsomer Murders*.

Bloom's character was a far cry from the upstanding, heroic parts he would go on to play. His role in the British crime show capitalized on his good looks. Bloom was cast as a love interest for two women, one of them married.

Bloom's character, Peter Drinkwater, is a womanizing burglar who is murdered. In addition to doing love scenes in the show, Bloom also had a chance to do a melodramatic death scene. Bloom's character meets a gruesome end, as he is killed with a pitchfork.

Although Bloom had trained to become an actor on the stage and had just been chosen to be part of the cast of a major movie, he was not too proud to consider television work when it came his way. He was simply happy to be paid for what he loved to do, and the young actor was not going to turn down the opportunity for paying work.

turing a part in the movie, as the idea of really getting a role in such a massive production might have overwhelmed him.

Bloom was reminded of his audition when he got a phone call telling him that the role of Faramir had gone to someone else. David Wenham would play Faramir, but Bloom was also told that Jackson had something different in mind for him. Jackson wanted Bloom to read for the part of Legolas Greenleaf, the elf warrior who plays an integral role in the story.

Jackson had been impressed by the tape Bloom had sent. He thought Bloom had the slender build, high cheekbones, and polished features he was looking for in the elf archer. He was especially awed by the amount of talent he had shown for someone so young. "The first time we saw Orlando, we rewound the tape, looked at him again, and then looked at each other," Jackson said. "He was straight out of drama school and hadn't done anything, but we knew we'd struck gold."[16]

The role of Legolas was much more prominent than that of Faramir, and Bloom was excited to be considered for it. He studied Tolkien's books and learned all he could about the character, and then did another reading on tape. Jackson came to Guildhall to talk with Bloom about the role, and his enthusiasm for the project made Bloom want the part even more. Two days before graduating with honors from Guildhall, he learned he had been chosen to play Legolas. "It was like winning the lottery!" Bloom exclaims. "Like having all your dreams fulfilled! It was amazing."[17]

The Next Stage

Bloom had expected to struggle to get parts and acting jobs. To have such a desirable part dropped at his feet just as he was leaving acting school was a fantastic surprise. He had received extensive training as an actor, but was not conceited about his talent. He knew he was still a novice and was excited and flattered to have been chosen for a large part in a major film. He had acted extensively onstage at Guildhall and in other school productions, but his professional work had been limited to a few small television roles and one part in a film. To be selected to participate in such a major project was a huge step for the young actor.

Riding on horseback and wielding a bloody sword, Bloom appears as Legolas in a scene from The Lord of the Rings.

Bloom was ready to accept the challenge. The accident he had suffered a little more than a year before had helped him focus his energies on his potential and made him appreciate the opportunities he had to act. He had trained for this since his teenage years and was eager to put his training to use. Before leaving for New Zealand to begin filming, Bloom walked through the woods near a friend's home in the country and imagined he was the elf Legolas, existing quietly in the timelessness of nature.

On to New Zealand

Bloom had always planned to go onstage and act in theatrical productions, but at age twenty-two he set aside those plans for the moment. He realized that *Rings* had the potential to launch the career he had been training for. His ability to nab small television, theater, and film roles and parts in school productions had shown him that he had the potential to make a go of an acting career. Now, he also had the potential to become a star.

Bloom would again be leaving familiar surroundings in pursuit of the career he chose. Since moving from Canterbury to London at sixteen, he had been intent on becoming an actor. He had taken risks and learned from them, both in the parts he played in theatrical productions and in the real-life challenges he had accepted. He left drama school feeling fortunate to be able to transition effortlessly from being a student to a professional actor beginning his career, and respected the challenges ahead.

Chapter 3

An Awesome Elf

A FEW MONTHS after graduating from drama school in 1999, Bloom was on an airplane, heading toward another turning point in this life. The young actor was on his way to New Zealand to spend eighteen months making a movie with a group of people he did not know. He was unsure of exactly what was ahead of him, but was happy to be part of such a major project.

In New Zealand, Bloom would immerse himself in his character and put to use the skills he had learned in drama school. He would discover new outlets for his adventurous energies, and a new group of friends to take part in them with him. He would fall in love with the culture and countryside of New Zealand while thoroughly enjoying his first major role as a professional actor.

On His Way

At twenty-two, Bloom was heading toward stardom, although he was not aware of the recognition that would be in store for him after the three *The Lord of the Rings* movies were released. He was simply grateful to have the opportunity to be part of such an exciting movie right after graduating from acting school.

The part of Legolas was everything Bloom had dreamed of as a child when he thought of being an actor. It contained adventure, excitement, and the physical challenges he thrived upon. "I mean, imagine being flown to this amazing country and being taught how to shoot a bow and arrow, learn to ride horses, and study swordplay—it was sick!" Bloom says. "I was pinching myself."[18]

Long-Term Commitment

Bloom's first acting job would not be an easy one, however. Jackson was taking a huge chance with *The Lord of the Rings*. Three epic films would follow the fellowship of nine comrades who travel across mythical Middle Earth to see that the powerful ring is destroyed in the pit of doom. Frodo Baggins is the hobbit who carries the ring, and is accompanied on his journey by a dwarf, humans, hobbits, and the elf archer, Legolas. Wanting to tell the story on a grand scale that did justice to the books, Jackson had worked to convince a studio to make the story in three films instead of one so that each of the novels in Tolkien's trilogy would have a film of its own. The project, which would cost $300 million, would mark the first time three separate movies were made in one continuous shoot. They would be released in 2001, 2002, and 2003.

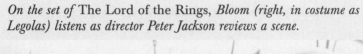

On the set of The Lord of the Rings, *Bloom (right, in costume as Legolas) listens as director Peter Jackson reviews a scene.*

Bloom and the other major actors in the movies would be in New Zealand for a year and a half, following an intense schedule. While the movies would include some amazing special effects generated by computer, at the heart of the movie would be the camaraderie and bonds of friendship among the major characters. To bring that fellowship across successfully on film would depend on how seriously the members of the cast approached their roles and how well they worked together.

Intimidating Experience

Bloom was flattered and excited to be part of such a huge undertaking, and he wanted to do justice to Jackson's vision of the film as well as to the fantasy Tolkien had created in *The Lord of the Rings* books. The enormity of what he was being asked to do was initially intimidating, however, especially after a visit to the set. Upon seeing row upon row of armor and weapons that would be used by the cast, he realized the breadth of the undertaking he would be part of.

Bloom appreciated Jackson's enthusiasm for the project and wanted to live up to the director's expectations. However, at the same time he was awed by the size of the project, and began to feel like an unqualified amateur in the company of so many experienced moviemakers. His neophyte status made him won-

Getting into Character

When taking on the part of Legolas, Bloom learned a few things about elves, and noted that the elves in Tolkien's novels are nothing like pixies or fairies. He became impressed with the wisdom they gather over a long lifetime. "Think about an elf—lives forever, can only die in battle or of a broken heart," he said in an interview for the article "The Making of an Epic" in *Entertainment Weekly*.

The other actors on the set sometimes teased Bloom about his good looks and Legolas's perfectly clean appearance. The actors who played the hobbits, and Viggo Mortensen, who played Aragorn, especially liked to tease Bloom. However, Bloom would good-naturedly give it back to them. When Mortensen called him "Elf boy," Bloom retorted, "Filthy human!"

der if he could hold his own on the screen with the other actors. In school he had been studying the work of Ian McKellen, who would play Gandolf. Now he was awed to be working with the actor, who had been made a knight by the queen of England.

Other *Rings* actors also brought years of experience to the set. Ian Holm, who played Bilbo, was an acclaimed theatrical actor and Academy Award nominee who had also been knighted. Christopher Lee, who would portray the evil Saruman, had made more than 250 movies. Some of the younger actors in the movie also had extensive resumes. The central character of Frodo would be played by Elijah Wood, who had been a child actor and had more than a dozen movies to his credit. Sean Astin, who played the hobbit Sam, had been acting professionally for more than ten years.

The *Rings* books are famed for their detailed depiction of a fantastic realm and epic struggles between the factions of good and evil. Like the pedigrees of his fellow actors, this literary legacy also eroded Bloom's confidence. Tolkien had even invented a language, Elvish, that Bloom would have to learn. The characters had been studied in literature classes for decades, and Bloom wondered how he would portray a character who already existed in the imaginations of so many readers. "Tolkien created the elves to be these perfect beings, to bring the world forward. It's quite a responsibility to take that to the screen,"[19] he said at the time.

In order to boost his confidence, Bloom gave himself a pep talk. He reasoned that he had been chosen for the part because he displayed some qualities that made him worthy to take on such a role. He was aware that he would need to approach his character seriously, but could not let that turn into a fear that kept him from allowing his acting ability to show through. He overcame his awe of his costars and began watching how they approached their roles, learning from what they were doing. Instead of being blocked by fear, he began to appreciate the opportunity to work with so many seasoned and acclaimed actors. He saw it as a way of continuing his education.

Getting into Character

Bloom quashed his insecurities by methodically approaching his role. He had several months to get ready, as such an ambitious project required some preparation by everyone involved. Filming would not begin until the cast had had time to get a feel for their characters and learn the skills they would need to use in their roles.

Before going on camera, Bloom spent several months training to take on the role of Legolas. He reread Tolkien's books, which he had begun reading when he was a teen, in order to get a sense of who his character was. He wanted to understand Legolas, to see how and why he reacts to situations the way he does. Because Legolas lives in a forest, Bloom also studied a book about trees.

Bloom then began to figure out simple things about Legolas, such as how he would stand and walk. Tolkien's elves are known for their inner calm, yet Legolas was a warrior, so Bloom determined that he would move like a samurai warrior, nimbly yet powerfully. When moving, he also concentrated on stalking like a cat, gracefully and steadily.

Legolas is an even-keeled yet physical character, who rides horses and participates in sword fights, yet does not explode with anger. Bloom had to figure out how to give his character an understated charisma and appeal. He needed to show his character's intensity and determination with a minimal amount of emotion.

Sharpening His Skills

Bloom also had to learn some new athletic skills before filming began. His character was an expert archer, so he not only had to learn to shoot a bow and arrow but to make it appear as if he had been doing so all his life. Soon after he arrived, a bow was placed into his hands, and he spent hours firing arrows to get the feel of the weapon. He became proficient enough that he could hit a paper plate that had been thrown up into the air.

Shooting a bow and arrow while on horseback was another skill Bloom had to acquire. He had ridden horses as a boy, but needed to learn to be able to show the grace people would expect of his character. He practiced until he had developed the riding posture and style that fit his character, and became comfortable with his horse galloping around the set. Echoing back to his broken bones of his younger years, he did have one injury. Bloom fell from a horse, landed on a rock, and broke three ribs, but otherwise remained healthy for the duration of the movie shoot.

Bloom also needed to bring Legolas's poised personality into his swordplay. He had trained in stage fighting while in

On the set, Bloom developed tremendous respect for Peter Jackson, who had a clear vision as to how Bloom should play the role of Legolas.

drama school, and received additional training from a fencing expert. He watched samurai movies to get a sense of their graceful and fluid yet powerful moves. "Being immortal, elves are very zenlike," he explains. "There's nothing chaotic about the way Legolas would fight—he'd never even get angry."[20]

Looking Like Legolas

Bloom not only had to display the skills of the fictional Legolas; he had to look like him. Bloom's features were modified on each day of filming as he spent two hours with the hair and makeup crew early in the morning. Pointy elf ears were applied and blue contacts covered his brown eyes. His hair was shaved into a mohawk to accommodate the long blond wig that gave him an ethereal appearance. The details of his physical transformation from human to elf were not made public in order to prevent too much information about the movie from leaking out before it was released. To keep his appearance a surprise for audiences, Bloom had to wear a hood while traveling to and from the set.

In addition to looking like one of Tolkien's elves, Bloom also had to sound like one. This required him to get a grip on the pronunciation and rhythms of Elvish, the language Tolkien had created for his books. Bloom had to deliver lines in Elvish on his first day of filming, and although it was not an easy scene for him, he managed to pull it off.

The outgoing Bloom had to quiet his personality to play the reserved Legolas. It is usually Legolas's job to sense danger and

Letting off Steam

Bloom developed a great deal of respect for Jackson, and said that it got to the point where he would believe anything the director told him about his character. However, shortly after filming began, Jackson hosted a party that made Bloom wonder about the director's common sense. "Pete lets off these fireworks and they all start flying into the crowd!" Bloom recalled in the *Entertainment Weekly* article "Making of an Epic" by Gillian Flynn. "He was running around like this mad scientist—and people were [screaming] Ahhhh! Pete was just standing there chuckling away, having a really good time. Everyone's like, Here we go—this guy's at the helm of this movie."

warn the others, or display his keen ability with a bow and arrow. Bloom's lines were usually short and sparse, and much of his character's feelings were conveyed with a look in his eyes or the ferocity with which he pulled back his bowstring. The part did not require Bloom to show great emotional depth, and that was fine with him. As a young actor fresh out of drama school, he was afraid he could not have done justice to a role that required more dialogue or emotion.

Bonding with Castmates

The camaraderie that evolved on the set made it easier for Bloom to tackle the challenges that came with his character. The rest of the cast also knew the importance of the film they were making and the huge amount of pressure there was to make the film a success, and they all appreciated what the others were going through. In addition, having the cast together in New Zealand during the long shooting schedule, as well as the picturesque location itself, helped generate a sense of community.

Bloom became close friends with the other members of the cast. The cast members played practical jokes on each other, including wrapping Bloom's trailer in duct tape. When the cast had a day off from shooting they often did things together in the countryside. Always up for a challenge, Bloom was attracted to the country's adventure sports and encouraged the others to join him. Bungee jumping became one of his favorite activities, and he went off the country's highest jump, a 134-meter (440-foot) fall, half a dozen times. The feeling of throwing himself into the air and falling through space with a giant rubber band attached to his feet satisfied his craving for excitement.

Bloom became especially close to Wood, Astin, Dominic Monaghan, and Billy Boyd, the actors who played the hobbits in *The Lord of the Rings*. With them, Bloom tried mountain biking and went white-water rafting. Bloom also tried skydiving and attempted to convince everyone to ride motocross bikes. Taking advantage of New Zealand's beaches, almost all of the members of the fellowship learned to surf. Bloom was often the one who came up with an adventurous plan and convinced the others to join him.

These adventurous activities helped Bloom feed the side of him that always wanted to push himself and try new things. "I didn't do it because I'm an adrenalin junkie," he says. "I did it because it's fun—I want to challenge myself and face my fears."[21]

Unlike the way he had taken risks while he was in drama school, however, Bloom made sure that he approached these activities with a measure of levelheadedness. He did not rush into things without thinking about them. Rather he planned activities that he knew he, and the others, would find thrilling. Bloom was often the instigator for the group's adventurous outings, but was careful not to push his limits to the point where he was likely to be injured.

Keeping Quiet

While Bloom was open about the friendships he formed with the other actors on the set, he was not forthcoming with the press about his personal life when it came to talking about girls he dated. He has acknowledged having a girlfriend during several months of the filming for *The Lord of the Rings* but did not name her. He attributes their breakup to the separation required by his work on the set in New Zealand.

British tabloids linked him to model Jemma Kidd, and said he had been engaged to her. Bloom would not confirm or deny the rumor. A girl he had been seeing while in drama school reportedly spent a month with him in New Zealand. Bloom remained quiet on the topic, although Monaghan noted that he and Bloom had enjoyed watching girls in New Zealand. "He's never had problems with the girls,"[22] Monaghan says.

Difficult Schedule

The cast appreciated the time they had away from the set, as it was limited. The movie's various scenes were filmed on fourteen locations throughout New Zealand, and the cast spent time traveling and getting into costume before they finally filmed a scene. One of the most difficult shots was the battle of Helm's Deep, which required three months of shooting at night under a

Liv Tyler and Bloom attend the London premiere of The Lord of the Rings *in December 2001. The movie's actors grew very close during filming.*

Offscreen Excitement

When the cast and crew of *The Lord of the Rings* had to move from New Zealand's North Island to South Island at the end of 1999, Bloom and Sean Bean found themselves in the middle of a real-life adventure. Bean, who played Boromir, hesitated to make a trip to the other island in a small airplane. Bloom agreed to drive with him and take the ferry over.

Their trip was delayed when Bloom stopped along the way to shop for Christmas presents just before a heavy rain caused landslides, which covered several roads. Bloom and Bean were trapped in a tiny town between two mud slides. They stayed there for a few days, until a helicopter could lift the pair out of the town and over to the movie set.

machine-induced downpour. Bloom and the others spent hours in the cold rain. "It was quite gruesome,"[23] Bloom says.

Another aspect of filming that made acting a challenge for Bloom and the others was that the scenes were not filmed in order. An actor might do a scene from the first movie one day, and the third the next. Because the tone of the movies gets gradually darker, this meant that Bloom and the other actors had to be especially careful that their characters' attitudes fit the tone of the particular scene being filmed. It was not always easy for Bloom to figure out where each scene fit in the trilogy, and he was impressed by Jackson's ability always to know where every scene fell in the flow of the three films.

A number of scenes were filmed in front of a blue screen. Many of the creatures and backgrounds seen in the film were not there when the actors were filmed, but were added later through special effects when the blue screen was edited out. This posed a challenge for the actors, who had to register expressions and physically react to magical or horrific things that were not there. Bloom and the others pretended to do battle against ferocious creatures called orcs and a troll that was represented as a foam cutout during filming. They also had to react to spirits in their midst that they could not see. Bloom relied on Jackson to tell him what his character would be seeing when the special effects were added in, to get an idea from the director about how his character was feeling.

Successful Approach

Making the movies was a test of Bloom's acting skill and maturity, and the young actor passed the test. The thoughtfulness Bloom and the other actors put into their characters and the camaraderie the cast enjoyed offscreen became apparent onscreen. Bloom captured the essence of his character's reserved yet commanding personality, and held up under the strain of months spent filming the movies' swordplay and battles.

Jackson liked what he saw of Bloom's swashbuckling nature. Bloom brought an added element of excitement to his battle scenes, running across the back of a troll in one of the films and sliding down a staircase on a shield in another. Bloom's initial intimidation about his character had been set aside, and he turned in a confident performance. His portrayal of Legolas, and the performances by the rest of the cast that traveled through Middle Earth to see that the powerful ring was destroyed, met with the approval of the movie's director. As filming ended, Jackson was enthusiastic about the work the cast had done in New Zealand.

Sad Farewell

The nine actors of the fellowship had formed a close bond, and had been so caught up in the day-to-day excitement of their work that it was difficult for them to realize that it was coming to an end. As the end of filming neared, Bloom encouraged the other eight members of the fellowship to get a tattoo of the number nine in Elvish. Bloom got one on his forearm in honor of his character's ability as an archer, and the others also agreed to get tattoos. This helped cement the bond that had grown among them during filming.

Filming ended with a farewell celebration. It was a fun, upbeat party, and included the stunt crew doing a traditional dance. However, it was tinged by sadness as well, as Jackson gave a farewell speech. It was an emotional good-bye, and Bloom did not want to let go. He knew that he would return to New Zealand over the next two years as the finishing touches were placed on the final two films, but would miss the strong bond that had grown among the actors while they made the

Peter Jackson and the cast of The Lord of the Rings *pose at a New York screening party. Bloom is second from right, standing.*

movies. "I hope I carry a part of [Legolas] with me forever," he says. "He's a special, special character and of course, my first. I'm never going to let go of him."[24]

Moving On

Bloom left the now-familiar islands of New Zealand to continue his career. He had arrived as a skilled but untested young actor, intimidated by the challenging project placed before him. He had proven to himself and others that he could hold his own on the screen with actors with much more experience, and that he had the maturity needed to approach such a difficult role in a methodical manner.

He had also had a good time while in New Zealand, establishing friendships he expects to keep for life. He made an impression on those he worked with, and shared with them his love for adventure. This helped bring the group close together, making the long project not only endurable but fantastically fun.

Bloom had turned in a strong performance, especially remarkable for an actor fresh out of drama school. However, it would take time for the movies to be released, and Bloom was not yet a recognizable actor. He did not think of himself as a movie star. However, his world had changed during the time he spent on the set of *The Lord of the Rings*. He had arrived in New Zealand as a skilled but untested actor, and left as a proven professional on the way to his next job.

Chapter 4

Hero and Heartthrob

BLOOM WAS LEAVING behind a close group of friends, a role he had embraced, and a director he had enjoyed working with. He was not yet an established actor, however, and had to look for more work. Although he had studied theatrical acting in drama school, he did not head to the stage after making *The Lord of the Rings*. He continued to look toward movies to provide him with the work that he had trained for.

Before long, Bloom would be seen as a hero and a heart-throb, thanks to his work in *Rings*. However, it would be months before the first of the three films in the trilogy would be seen by the public. After filming was completed, Jackson and the movie's editors went through a rigorous postproduction process to combine the live-action footage with the computer-generated scenes. They also had to cut the movie down to a length appropriate for commercial theaters. Bloom would remain an anonymous actor for a few more months while his breakout film was readied for release.

Black Hawk Down

While *The Lord of the Rings* was being completed in the first part of 2001, Bloom was offered work in a number of teen movies. However, he did not want to take roles that mainly emphasized his good looks. He wanted meatier parts that would allow him to learn in front of the camera.

He found what he was looking for with the war movie *Black Hawk Down*, which chronicles the 1993 conflict between the U.S. military and a Somalian warlord in which eighteen U.S.

Bloom poses at the London premiere of the 2002 war movie Black Hawk Down *in which he plays the role of a soldier who breaks his back.*

soldiers and more than one hundred Somalis were killed. Bloom would play the part of a soldier who breaks his back. While he was auditioning for the part he mentioned that he had also suffered a back-breaking injury, and that as he was recuperating he was in the hospital next to a soldier with a paralyzing injury. "It's surreal how life has these patterns,"[25] he notes.

Bloom's character, PFC Todd Blackburn, is injured when he falls 70 feet (21.34m) from a helicopter; his evacuation for medical treatment poses grave difficulties for his unit. The character is not on-screen for long, but that did not matter to Bloom. He was happy to get a role in the movie because it would give him the opportunity to work with director Ridley Scott, who had directed *Alien*. Although he only had a few lines in the movie, and would do little with Scott other than be thrown out of a helicopter by him, Bloom still looked forward to the chance to meet the seasoned and respected director. Bloom was a talented actor but not yet well known, since the first *Rings* movie had not yet been released. He counted himself fortunate to be able to work with a famous director.

The Lord of the Rings Release

Bloom finished his work on *Black Hawk Down* in fall 2001, and soon was making publicity appearances in advance of the release of *The Lord of the Rings: The Fellowship of the Ring*, the first movie in the trilogy. Bloom appeared on several British television shows, as well as MTV's *Total Request Live*.

The movies generated a great deal of speculation, as fans of the books debated whether or not they would live up to the prerelease hype surrounding the films. One person who was pleased was Jackson, whose high expectations had been fulfilled by his solid cast and creative special effects. The first film was met with glowing reviews by critics who saw it as a masterpiece. "*The Lord of the Rings: The Fellowship of the Ring* is thrilling—a great picture, a triumphant picture, a joyfully conceived work of cinema,"[26] wrote reviewer Lisa Schwarzbaum.

When Bloom saw the completed product for the first time, he was stunned. He could not believe he had been part of a project that had produced such an epic film. It was surreal to be watching himself on-screen, wearing a blond wig and elf ears, in a movie that was so captivating, entertaining, and admired by audiences.

From Obscurity to Stardom

The release of the movie quickly took away Bloom's anonymity as the twenty-four-year-old actor went from obscurity to stardom. Moviegoers were initially surprised that the blond-haired, blue-eyed elf in the film actually had dark hair and brown eyes, and some of the first magazine covers featuring him showed him in his *Rings* attire. However, fans soon accepted him for his brown-eyed, dark-haired self.

The fans who admired Bloom in *Lord of the Rings* also wanted to know more about him. With *Rings* as his first major movie, and his previous appearances limited to plays and television shows in Britain, there was an aura of mystery about the new star. People began searching for more information on the Internet, and beginning on February 27, 2002, he held the number one search spot on the Internet Movie Database for eight weeks.

Bloom was soon cited as one of the most popular young newcomers to the screen, and a fresh face to be admired by teenage girls. Fans devoted Web sites to him, and in summer 2002, he was named to *Teen People*'s list of "25 Hottest Stars Under 25" as the "hottest adventurer." He was also named one

Another World

Bloom's polite manners and preference for costume dramas really made him seem like a romantic hero from another time. "There is something old-fashioned about him," wrote Allison Glock in *GQ*. "He is courtly and sweetly naïve." Bloom had a humble, kind attitude, noted Michele Hatty in *USA Weekend*. "He's the type of guy who will put a cashmere wrap around a visitor's shoulders if she looks cold."

Even Bloom himself said he sometimes felt like he belonged in a different world. "I do feel like I'm from another time," he told Glock. "I can hardly use my phone. I'm computer-illiterate. I use a pencil and paper. It slows me down, but I really do prefer it."

of *YM*'s "20 Hottest Guys." By this time he had also appeared in a Gap ad, which showed him running from fans.

Bloom received attention for his talent as well as his looks. He won a 2002 Empire Award for Best Debut, and a 2002 MTV Movie Award for Best Breakthrough Star. Although *Teen People* pegged him as a star mainly on the basis of his looks, he had told the interviewer about his back-breaking accident and his love for extreme sports, also revealing that, "I like films that have integrity and a great story. But I also see myself doing comedy because I think people find me amusing. I can be a bit geeky, which is what people don't expect."[27]

The attention took Bloom by surprise, as he had not expected to establish a huge fan base with his role as Legolas. He had become an actor not to gain fame, but because he liked to act. The adoration of fans that came with it was a shock. "The goal

At the 2002 Hollywood premiere of The Lord of the Rings: The Two Towers, *Bloom signs autographs for his legions of fans.*

was to get paid as an actor," he says. "That would have been enough."[28]

That Special Something

Bloom's good looks were part of the reason for his appeal, as evidenced by the number of teen girls who began wearing "I (heart) Orlando" T-shirts, but in addition Bloom had an understated charisma that came across on-screen. "He's in the long tradition of guys like James Dean and Russell Crowe," says Gregor Jordan, who would direct Bloom in his next movie, *Ned Kelly.* "There's just something about him that makes people want to sit in the dark and watch him on a movie screen."[29]

Another director said Bloom's natural good looks make him appear as if he could have come from another time. In addition, Bloom's attitude is unwaveringly polite when he meets with fans and the press. He graciously submits to interviews, signs autographs, and once helped an elderly man whose wheelchair had broken down. Bloom is a gentleman, as well as a talented actor, and his thoughtful, considerate attitude toward others has made people think highly of him.

Staying Grounded

Bloom was determined not to let the attention he was receiving change him. He did not want to become pompous or egotistical because of all the interest in him. He got help in this regard from his sister, who was thinking of attending acting school herself, as well as from a cousin who worked as an art director. They would not allow Bloom's sudden fame to go to his head. They reminded Bloom of his roots, where he had come from, and the little he had done to deserve special treatment. He appreciated their honesty.

In any event, ever since drama school, the challenge of acting had been more appealing to him than the attention he drew for it. "I never really wanted to be famous," he says. "I trained for three years at drama school to be an actor—not a celebrity."[30]

One person who was impressed with how Bloom handled the attention was Jackson, Bloom's director in *Rings.* After

Bloom became the center of a great deal of attention following the movie's release, Jackson noted that the young actor had not changed much. He remained the same adventurous and upbeat person Jackson had come to know on the *Rings* set.

Love Interest

Although Bloom did not actively pursue his heartthrob status, many young girls had a crush on him. Bloom speculated that the attention he generated had something to do with the nonthreatening nature of his character. He was handsome but not domineering, cute without being too pushy. "Legolas is a good, safe guy for girls to pin their dreams on,"[31] he says.

The increased interest in Bloom included questions about his love life. However, he declined to talk about his girlfriends and did not make his dating life public. Such reticence, or discretion, only fueled speculation, however. He was linked to actress Christina Ricci after being seen with her at a party, although neither of them said anything about dating.

In 2003 Bloom met an actress whom he would quietly date for several years. Kate Bosworth had starred in the surfing movie *Blue Crush*, and she and Bloom began seeing each other regularly. However, neither offered details to the press of their relationship.

Career Choices

In addition to focusing increased attention on his background and personal life, Bloom's role in *The Lord of the Rings* was bringing him more offers of acting roles. He now felt a new sense of responsibility, which he had not anticipated at this point in his career. Until this time, Bloom had been thankful for the parts that came his way and had few choices to make. It had been an easy decision for him to choose to take a role in *The Lord of the Rings* and work with Scott in *Black Hawk Down*. However, as more roles were offered to him he had to think about which direction he wanted to take his career. He wanted to be a serious actor rather than a teen idol. His looks garnered attention, but he had to make people notice his talent as an actor.

Glimpses of Bloom as a Boyfriend

Bloom rarely offers details of his relationships with women, but observers have gleaned a few insights into what he would be like as a boyfriend. For example, he once flew to Dubai to be with a girl he was dating, and another time sent an Irish girl an airplane ticket to get her to visit him. "When you're with me it's exciting, fun and very full-on," he told Nick Webster of the British newspaper *Mirror*. "At the same time, I'm easy going. But all that depends on what girl I'm with."

He also noted that he loved the feeling of being in love. "When you start falling for somebody and you can't stop thinking about when you're going to see them again, I love that," he said in a *Teen People* article in December 2002. He added that "women are beautiful. They deserve to be cherished and respected," although he also said that "they're a handful."

He said the way he treats women is influenced by how he has seen his sister treated by her boyfriends. "I'm quite sensitive to women," he told Allison Glock in *GQ*. "I saw how my sister got treated by her boyfriends. I read this thing that said when you are in a relationship with a woman, imagine how you would feel if you were her father. That's been my approach, for the most part."

Bloom accompanies girlfriend Kate Bosworth in 2004 at the premiere of one of her movies.

Costar Heath Ledger is shown with Bloom in this movie still from Ned Kelly, *an Australian film that did poorly at the box office.*

Bloom could have signed on for roles that took advantage of his heartthrob status and would concentrate on his looks rather than his acting ability, or he could try to stretch his acting ability with a variety of parts. Bloom knew in his heart that he wanted to have a career that allowed him to grow as an actor and take on many different roles, but he hoped he would not be too tempted by the money that came with roles that emphasized his good looks. As he weighed his options, Bloom said he hoped his popularity with young girls would not keep him from making interesting movie choices.

Ned Kelly

In keeping with his desire to try new things, Bloom chose a western-style movie for his next role. *Ned Kelly* tells the legendary story of an Irish-Australian outlaw in Australia in the late 1800s. Heath Ledger had the title role, while Bloom played his best friend.

Bloom worked on the movie in early 2002 and again brought his considerable talent to the role. He was lauded for his performance, but the picture itself was criticized as being plodding when it was released in Australia and Britain in 2003. It was made available to audiences in the United States the next year, but failed to catch on in America. "Australia's devotion to its most famous 19th-century outlaw is likely to remain a mystery to non-Aussies, despite the exertions of Ned Kelly,"[32] wrote reviewer Schwarzbaum. She did, however, say that Bloom gave an "effortlessly charismatic" performance, outshining Ledger whenever both were on-screen at the same time.

Although *Ned Kelly* garnered few good reviews, its lackluster showing did little to hurt Bloom's career. The second installment of *The Lord of the Rings* had been released at the end of 2002 and had resulted in another round of compliments for Bloom in his role as Legolas. In addition, on the set of *Ned Kelly*, Bloom met actor Geoffrey Rush, who was reading the script for *Pirates of the Caribbean* and encouraged Bloom to consider a part in the picture.

The Calcium Kid

While he was mulling over *Pirates*, Bloom committed to making a movie in his home country. In fall 2002 he began making *The Calcium Kid*, a mockumentary, or parody of a documentary, made in London. He played a milkman who becomes a boxer after his voluminous calcium intake makes his bones incredibly strong.

Bloom had the starring role in the movie, and he believed he could identify with his character: "Jimmy is an everyday geezer. He's not trying to be anything. In fact, he's just like me."[33] Bloom liked being able to understand easily where the character was coming from; he was also attracted to the movie because it gave him an opportunity to take a role with more dialogue than he had been given in the past. In addition, working in England gave Bloom the chance to be home again. He could see old friends while he enjoyed acting in London.

Having the leading role gave him the opportunity to test his ability to carry a film. He did not want his first starring role to be in an extravagant production because he did not want the responsibility of trying to make a multimillion-dollar picture successful. He was attracted to the low-budget movie because it gave him the chance to take the reins of a movie without having too much at stake. He could experiment and be creative without obsessing about what would happen if things did not turn out well.

While Bloom was proud of the work he did for *The Calcium Kid*, its release was delayed until April 2004. When it finally hit theaters, it did not stay long and did not generate good reviews. Bloom believed in the movie and the work he had done for it, but audiences were unimpressed.

Bigger and Better

After making *The Calcium Kid*, Bloom again carefully evaluated the roles he was offered. His career was on the rise after the

Bloom appears in his first starring role in the mockumentary film The Calcium Kid, *the story of a milkman who becomes a boxer.*

release and stellar reviews of the first two movies in *The Lord of the Rings* series. He wanted to keep working, but was choosy about the roles he took. He wanted to make sure the movies he made were projects he could learn from.

Bloom had made a statement about the type of career he was establishing with the roles he accepted after *Rings*. Although he had received a great deal of attention from young girls after *The Lord of the Rings: The Fellowship of the Ring* was released, he did not capitalize on his good looks with lighthearted, teen-oriented fare. Instead, he had chosen a war movie, an Australian outlaw film, and a small British movie for his next projects. Bloom had graduated from drama school, but did not want to stop learning as he continued to pursue roles that intrigued him. Now he was ready to move quietly on to much bigger projects, ones that would allow him to work again with acclaimed directors and learn from established stars.

Chapter 5

Working with the Best

AFTER WORKING ON several smaller movies following the epic *The Lord of the Rings*, Bloom was again chosen for big-budget fare when he got roles in *Pirates of the Caribbean: The Curse of the Black Pearl* and *Troy*. He did not agree to make the movies because of their multimillion-dollar price tags, however. He took the offers because they gave him a chance to work with stars and directors he could learn from.

In the pictures, Bloom was happy to play a major supporting role rather than the lead. This gave him solid exposure but did not place the success of the movies on his shoulders. In addition, he was able to work with and learn from stars such as Johnny Depp and Brad Pitt.

Easy Choice

Jerry Bruckheimer, a famous producer of action movies, had worked with Bloom on *Black Hawk Down*. He remembered the young actor when he was producing *Pirates of the Caribbean* and it came time to choose a cast for the movie. After finishing *Ned Kelly*, Bloom was asked to meet *Pirates of the Caribbean* director Gore Verbinski for dinner. Also in attendance was Keira Knightley, and when Verbinski saw the two of them together he immediately knew they would be perfect as the love-struck couple in *Pirates*. "I just kept looking at them across the table and thought, 'This could work,'"[34] Verbinski says.

When he was approached with the idea of trying out for a role in the movie, Bloom had initially been reluctant to consider it. At that point in his career he had been looking for small, interesting roles that would let him polish his acting ability, and this movie was anything but small. The $125-million picture, based on the popular attraction at Disneyland, contained a stellar cast, offered dazzling special effects, and would be shot on location around the world. However, Geoffrey Rush, who worked with Bloom in *Ned Kelly* and had the role of an evil pirate in the movie, told Bloom he would regret it if he did not give the role a try.

Once Bloom learned more about the movie, it was easy for him to say yes to the role of Will Turner. He would have a chance to show off the fencing skills he had learned for *The Lord*

In the wildly successful Pirates of the Caribbean, *Bloom landed the role of Will Turner. He is shown here with costar Keira Knightley.*

of the Rings and again take part in an adventure movie. After
making movies that were released first in Australia and Britain,
he would have the opportunity with *Pirates* to make a statement
with a big film in the American movie market. In addition, he
would be acting opposite Depp and looked forward to working
closely with the acclaimed actor. "Knowing that Johnny Depp
was involved in this movie made it a no-brainer for me," Bloom
says. "Johnny is such a hero of mine. As a kid, I'd run to his
movies."[35]

Pirates

Bloom had been the last lead to be chosen for the movie.
Verbinski had been looking for an actor who could hold his own
on the screen with the charismatic Depp. As Will Turner, Bloom
would need to make it clear that he was the best man for
Knightley's Elizabeth Swann, and keep audiences from wonder-
ing why she did not fall for Depp.

Bloom played a strong romantic lead in *Pirates* and was a
handsome, stalwart contrast to Depp's flamboyant and gritty
Jack Sparrow. Depp let Bloom be the hero who gets the girl,
while he gave a broad performance of a drunken yet clever and
crafty pirate. Their characters complement each other well, as
they rescue Knightley from an evil pirate played by Rush. Along
the way, the movie is filled with action and special effects as
pirates turn to skeletons in the moonlight, sword fights ensue,
and shipboard battles boom across the screen.

The role turn out to be perfect for Bloom. It allowed him
to fulfill a childhood fantasy of being a pirate, show off his
sword-fighting ability, and capitalize on his good looks. "It's all
that fun, swashbuckling stuff, which is a good laugh," Bloom
says. "I loved the boat-to-boat battles and all the swinging on
ropes."[36]

Learning as He Goes

Pirates gave Bloom the opportunity both to enjoy its action-
oriented scenes and to play a character who evolves during the
course of the picture. Will Turner works as a blacksmith but

Surprising Star

When Bloom began to garner attention after the release of the *The Lord of the Rings* movies and was then chosen to star alongside Johnny Depp in *Pirates of the Caribbean*, his family and friends were surprised by his sudden fame. Fans were taking note of Bloom's handsome features and steadfast portrayal of Legolas, but to his family and friends he was still Orli. His childhood and young adult years had seemed so ordinary that his mother had not expected him to achieve such a measure of fame from his work.

While she was surprised by how well known her son was becoming, she was also proud of the way he was handling the attention. He still

kept in touch with his mother via phone calls, and they maintained their close relationship. "I really do admire him tremendously, how he's coping, because he is so grounded and doesn't let it affect him," she said in a BBC News interview in 2003.

Although Bloom's work in the Pirates of the Caribbean *cemented his popularity with audiences, the actor remained modest and down-to-earth.*

learns that his father was a pirate, and has to solve an identity crisis as he decides whether at heart he is a blacksmith or a pirate. As the movie progresses, Bloom has to show his character coming to an understanding of who he is and what he is meant to do with his life.

The movie gave Bloom the opportunity to play a character with more emotional depth than he had in past major roles, and also gave him the chance to learn acting techniques from Depp. He watched how Depp played against his good looks and developed the flamboyant Sparrow's character. He respected Depp's

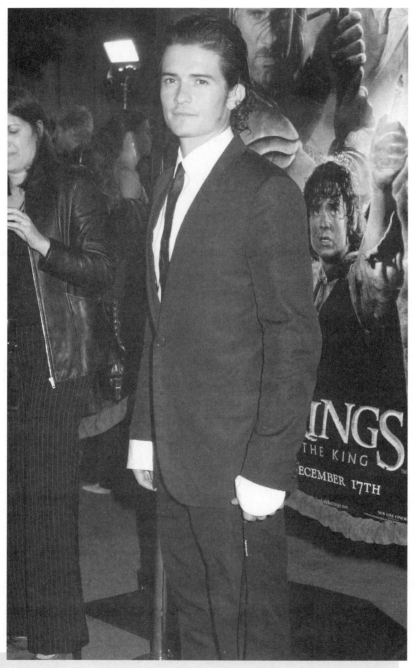

Bloom appears at the premiere of The Return of the King, *the final and most acclaimed film of* The Lord of the Rings *trilogy.*

acting and admired his fearlessness. "He's so courageous in how he develops a character and puts himself out there," Bloom says. "He's not afraid to fall on his face."[37]

Depp gave Bloom career advice as well as acting tips, telling him not to chase after money but to follow his heart. Bloom admired the way Depp had managed to stay true to himself as he navigated his career, and how gracious he was in helping the younger actor. "He surpassed all my expectations as a human being, let alone as an actor,"[38] Bloom says.

Bloom also earned the respect of director Verbinski while making the movie, as his unassuming, approachable manner came across well on-screen. Bloom was someone people could relate to. Part of this was because he felt so ordinary himself. It was still hard for him to grasp what it meant to be a star, and he did not want to admit to himself that he was a celebrity. He preferred to concentrate on the work at hand, maintain his long-standing friendships, and try not to let his ego get in the way.

Top-Notch Movies

Bloom tried to approach his acting roles by bringing out the human element, finding something that people could identify with in his character. While he acknowledged that he might modify this approach in the future, it worked for *Pirates*, which was a hit with audiences when it was released in the summer of 2003. Like the Disneyland ride it was named after, *Pirates* had a scary yet humorous feel to it.

Some reviewers thought the movie was too showy and relied too much on special effects and exaggerated acting. However, others thought it was a great way to bring back the exciting adventure of pirate movies. "This is an original work in an antique mood," said reviewer Richard Corliss. "The actors and authors all have fun with the genre without making fun of it."[39]

Regardless of what reviewers thought, audiences loved it. Bloom's career received a boost from *Pirates*, and two sequels were eventually commissioned. His career was also helped by the release of the final installment of *The Lord of the Rings* in

December 2003. *The Lord of the Rings: The Return of the King* received even more acclaim than the first two had, as reviewers heralded it as one of the greatest movie-making feats of all time. In March 2004 *The Return of the King* earned eleven Academy Awards, including Best Picture and Best Director for Jackson.

Bloom now had two more hits to his credit, although he was not the main character in either film. Depp's flamboyant turn as pirate Jack Sparrow had captured most of the *Pirates* buzz, and Viggo Mortensen and Elijah Wood played the characters who made the biggest transformations in *Rings*. Still, Bloom's performance was noted and appreciated by audiences, and he soon received a new opportunity to shine in another major, big-budget movie.

Bloom continued to put himself in position for roles in movies that were not standard comedies or dramas. He made it known that he was interested in doing something different with each picture, and felt fortunate when he was able to get roles that helped him fulfill this career objective. He did not go for Hollywood movies that followed a formula designed only to bring people to the theater. He also did not pursue big-money offers for movies he did not consider to be projects he could learn from. He chose to do movies that both interested and challenged him.

Troy

Although Bloom was always looking to improve as an actor, it was his popularity rather than his acting ability that first impressed director Wolfgang Peterson when he began considering Bloom for a role in a forthcoming epic to be called *Troy*. Peterson, the director of *The Perfect Storm* and *Das Boot*, saw a crowd of teenage girls going crazy for Bloom outside the hotel where he was waiting to talk to the actor. He realized he was dealing with someone with a huge fan base, who could put an audience into the seats in a theater. Peterson worked quickly to bring Bloom into the project.

Troy was based on the ancient Greek story of the Trojan War. The battles begin after Paris goes to Greece on a peace mission

Home Base

After Bloom graduated from drama school in 1999, he spent much of the next few years traveling around the world to various movie shoot locations. He was in New Zealand for *The Lord of the Rings* and Australia for *Ned Kelly*. Then he was off to the island of St. Vincent for *Pirates of the Caribbean* and Mexico and Malta for *Troy*.

Bloom did not stay in one place for long, but still remembered his English roots. He kept his belongings at his mother's house until he got his own place in London in 2003, furnishing it with things he bought on his travels. A few years later he described his home as bohemian and chaotic, almost like a warehouse for him to store the things he bought while traveling. "It is definitely in need of attention and love," he said in *USA Weekend*.

Although his job kept him busy traveling, he said he would always consider England his home. "I'll always keep myself rooted in London and England, because I love my home and I love Brits," he said in an interview with Nick Webster for the British newspaper *Mirror*. "Culturally, I'm so different to Americans, whereas with Brits I get it, I get everything. When they're being funny, I get it. And I feel like I'm at home."

Bloom added that one of the perks of his job was having enough money to be able to treat his friends to a nice meal, or to send them an airplane ticket so they could come and see him when they were on vacation. He liked having his old friends around him, to keep his fame from going to his head. "In terms of grounding you, it's good to have those people around," he told Webster. "That's why I bought a place in London. That's where my mates are and I know I need to have those people around just to keep my head straight."

but raises the ire of the Greeks when he takes Helen, the wife of the Greek king Menelaus, with him when he returns to Troy. Bloom was familiar with the story from the play *The Trojan Women*, which he had performed while in drama school. In that story, he had played Menelaus, the husband of Helen, who is killed in the movie version but survives the war in the classic play. This time he would be playing Paris, the man who takes Helen away. Another difference this time around was that the story would be told on a considerably larger scale. The movie, with a $175-million budget, would be filmed in Malta, Mexico, and London.

Diane Kruger plays Helen alongside Bloom as Paris in Troy, *the epic movie about the Trojan War.*

The movie has a stellar cast: Brad Pitt in the role of the Greek commander Achilles, who goes into battle in order to obtain honor and have his name live forever; Eric Bana as Hector, the heroic Trojan warrior; the acclaimed Peter O'Toole as King Priam, the father of Paris and Hector. Bloom, as Paris, must decide whether to fight for the love of his life or avoid the battles in order to be with her.

Understanding Paris

With the role of Paris, Bloom was faced with an interesting dilemma. He wanted to make audiences understand the motivations of his character, whose love and selfishness start a war, and who then lacks the bravery to put his life on the line. "I had a big moral struggle with it," Bloom said. "Everyone would like to say death and honor—at least as a guy—but Paris chooses love and life. . . . It's an intimidating thing, to make an audience understand what you're doing—so they don't completely loathe you."[40]

In *Pirates* and *The Lord of the Rings*, Bloom had played upstanding characters audiences found it easy to cheer for. Paris is more of an antihero, and Bloom had to find a way to make audiences understand the character and his motives. Next to the fame-hungry Achilles and the upright Hector, Paris comes off as a selfish and immature, although romantic, character. Bloom found it a challenge to get audiences to appreciate the motives of a character who offers to fight, but when faced with death runs to his brother for protection. In addition, with the huge sets and massive battle scenes, he also had to make sure Paris would not get lost in the action in the epic war film.

Peterson allowed Bloom to approach the character his own way and bring his own ideas to the role. Bloom appreciated the opportunity to do some experimenting. Although he liked Peterson's directing style, he also realized that the director would have the final say about which scenes made it into the movie and which did not. "He's open to what you think your character should do," Bloom says. "He humors us: You do your cute little acting thing and if I don't like it I'll cut it! Fair enough, that works."[41]

Learning from Brad

Bloom also learned a few things from his costar Pitt, although the lessons were learned more offscreen than on. Bloom was a star, but the attention he received from fans was minor compared to the notice received by Pitt. Pitt had been starring in movies and captivating audiences since the early 1990s, and his actress troubled marriage to Jennifer Aniston had been heavily scrutinized by the media. Along the way he had learned how to deal with fans and the media, and Bloom watched Pitt for tips on handling crowds.

Pitt was recognized wherever he went, and Bloom found the effect that he had on other people to be a bit scary. However, Pitt knew how to deal with the attention. Bloom watched as Pitt handled a mob of photographers and fans who met them when they went out to eat. Pitt did not get addled or ruffled but kept his composure and moved away from the crowd. From Pitt, Bloom learned to deal with the additional attention that came with being a film star, as well as how to deflect it.

Bloom had not yet reached Pitt's level of fame, however. While he was a popular film star, people did not always recognize him in public. When they did, he was not opposed to stopping to chat and pose for a picture. When Bloom was filming *Troy* in Malta, he helped one woman figure out how to use her camera when she took her children to see him. He even offered to take a second picture in case the first did not turn out.

Novelty Wears Off

Although Bloom still did not get the same kind of response as Pitt did when he appeared in public, he was well aware that he was living a life very different from the norm. His career had been moving steadily upward since the release of the first *Rings* film, and his life was filled with travel to exotic locations for movie shoots, interviews with reporters, and the consideration of scripts for new projects. The hectic pace had been exciting at first, but was quickly becoming routine.

Bloom's schedule since leaving drama school had consisted mainly of making movies back-to-back; in addition, he was traveling all over the world to do his job. While filming *Troy* in Malta in summer 2003, he sometimes felt burdened by his unusual, irregular lifestyle. He even felt homesick while he was away from London making the movie. The novelty of fame that had come with the release of *The Lord of the Rings* had worn off for Bloom, and the travel that came with acting was turning the job he loved into drudgery.

His busy schedule made Bloom appreciate the little time he had to himself. He was happy to have time to take a walk on the beach, or be with his girlfriend, Bosworth. While Bloom's full schedule made his life far from easy, he also realized he had little to gripe about. He had the career he had dreamed of and was living a life many people would love to lead. "I'm 26," he said.

"I'm in the prime of my life. What do I have to complain about?"[42]

Bloom also enjoyed getting together with old friends, but preferred meeting them in secluded places where they could talk rather than visiting a crowded club. He had had enough of the club scene in his school days, and now was more interested in being with his friends than in going to a place filled with strangers. He and his costars from *Rings* or friends from his school days still got together and stayed out late, enjoying the time they had to spend with each other.

Times like that were not plentiful for Bloom as he continued to make film after film. In a career that had begun only a few years earlier, Bloom had experienced moviemaking on both a

Brad Pitt and Bloom are shown at the 2004 Cannes Film Festival. From his Troy *costar, Bloom learned how to deflect unwanted attention from fans.*

grand and small scale. Learning from each role he played, Bloom chose his parts based on the director, his costars, and what the role could teach him. While he had been broadening his personal repertoire since his role as Legolas, he knew there were still many more types of roles he could consider that would turn him into an even more well-rounded actor. After successfully being part of big-budget movies such as *Pirates* and *Troy*, Bloom was poised to take more chances with his career.

Chapter 6

Orlando Blooms

BLOOM CONTINUED TO juggle his busy schedule and the adoration of his fans, and tried to do so without becoming conceited or letting all the attention affect him. Bloom had the looks, talent, and the right attitude to keep propelling his career forward. He approached his career in a thoughtful manner, without letting his ego make decisions for him.

To help him keep a level head in what could be a crazy business, Bloom continued to keep his personal life closely guarded. He knew he could not avoid the press duties that came along with being a star, and politely answered questions from the media. However, he kept the conversations focused on things related to movies and his career.

Bloom's career had become a demanding one, and he was on location making movies much more often than he was home in England. He was not excited about all of the traveling he had to do for the movies he was in, but he still loved acting and did not want to give up the opportunities that came his way. He wanted to continue to advance his career and become a better actor, even if it meant making some personal sacrifices. A popular actor on the verge of becoming a superstar, he wanted to continue to build on the momentum of his career.

Troy Disappoints

Bloom was a hot enough star that his popularity was barely affected by the mediocre reviews *Troy* received when it was released in May 2004. So much had been expected from the big-budget movie that even though it brought people to theaters, it was not considered

The Trojan horse from Troy *is used to promote the film in Tokyo. The movie fared poorly at American box offices.*

a success. The movie had style and an epic grandness to it, but that was not enough to captivate audiences. "Although Troy isn't as wooden as the giant horse the Greek army used to invade the titular city 3,200 years ago, neither does it gallop along with speed or grace,"[43] wrote reviewer Leah Rozen in *People* magazine.

Rozen said that Bloom's Paris is a more captivating character than Pitt's Achilles, writing, "Pitt is blond and bland" but adding that Bloom; Bana as his brother, Hector; and O'Toole as King Priam were "more engaging."[44] However, reviewer Todd McCarthy questioned the chemistry between Bloom and Diane Kruger as Helen. He noted that the feelings they have for each other hardly seem worth waging a war. "[The] relationship between her and Paris seems like no more than a lusty diversion for both even at its peak, hardly the sort of passion that might result in the deaths of thousands and the ruin of a city,"[45] McCarthy said.

Bloom had struggled with the character of Paris, playing him as a love-struck prince who wants to fight but lacks courage in battle, and had found it difficult to come to grips with his character's selfish motivations. Although he tried to bring across his character's anxiety over his cowardly and self-serving choices and redeem him by playing him stalwartly shooting an arrow into Achilles' heel, his Paris comes across as little more than wimpy.

Actor and Producer

Although Bloom received little critical acclaim for his role in *Troy*, most of the criticism for the film itself revolved around the movie's special effects, which were seen as overbearing, and Pitt's brooding portrayal of Achilles. Bloom's popularity allowed him to escape much of the movie's criticism. The following summer, he was named the sexiest actor in Britain, as well as one of *People* magazine's "50 Hottest Bachelors."

While Bloom appreciated the compliments, he did not want to be seen merely as a heartthrob. Like Pitt and Depp, he wanted to take roles that played against his good looks and allowed him to develop a character's personality. To that end, Bloom took a break after the epic with a small, interesting role, the kind

Jewelry Tells a Story

Bloom carries memories from the movies he has made and the places he has traveled on a string around his neck. In the article, "Oh What a Knight!," in *People* magazine, he called the necklace his "life on a string." In an interview with Allison Glock for *GQ*, he noted that the necklace contains a key ring he received as a gift from Johnny Depp after they made *Pirates* together, as well as a piece of greenstone from Billy Boyd, who played a hobbit in *The Lord of the Rings*. It also has as a handcuff key from New York City, a shell he found on a beach in Thailand, and a silver ball from Tokyo. "I've always kept all these funny little things, even as a kid," he told Glock. "These things fill up my heart. If I were ever to lose them, I'd be really devastated. Isn't that pathetic?"

that would give him room for experimentation. He quietly moved on after *Troy* to the set of *Haven*, which he both acted in and coproduced.

Bloom began making *Haven* at the end of 2003, and traveled to the Cayman Islands in the West Indies to make the independent film. The low-budget picture was a far cry from the historical epics he had become known for. It did not have a huge cast, and Bloom's costars were Bill Paxton and Gabriel Byrne. Frank E. Flowers, who had grown up in the Cayman Islands and majored in film at the University of Southern California, wrote the script and was making his debut as a director with *Haven*.

In the contemporary movie, Bloom plays a character named Shy, a British man who gets involved with a pair of underhanded businessmen. The criminals, played by Paxton and Byrne, flee to the islands to avoid being prosecuted by the law. Bloom's character gets caught up in their scheme and suffers disheartening consequences as a result. *Haven* gave Bloom the opportunity to try something with a more modern and edgy feel than his previous pictures.

In addition to giving him a new type of role, the movie gave Bloom the opportunity to try something new offscreen. Bloom was a coproducer of the film and had input into how the movie was made. "It's the first time I've done that," he says. "In terms of the role that I've been playing as a producer, it's been really just a sounding board; it's very much a collaborative effort."[46]

The movie was not well received and was criticized for being confusing. Although Bloom was praised for a tender love scene and for a fight scene in which his character has acid thrown on his face, he could not save a movie whose writer had failed to tie the movie's many subplots together. "The presence of Orlando Bloom . . . may attract a teen audience, but the foundation of fans Bloom's built on the basis of 'The Lord of the Rings' trilogy and 'Pirates of the Caribbean' will find far shakier shelter here,"[47] wrote *Variety* reviewer Eddie Cockrell.

The movie was shown at the Toronto International Film Festival in September 2004, but was not widely distributed. Bloom had taken part in the picture for the opportunity to have a different type of role and dabble in movie production. While it gave him the chance to learn more about moviemaking, it was more of a fun diversion for him than a major career stepping-stone.

Kingdom of Heaven

After taking a break from big-budget pictures with *Haven*, Bloom had the opportunity to return to the cinematic spectacles that had become the hallmark of his career. Although he had made himself a promise that after *Troy* he would avoid movies with swords and horses, he could not pass up a role in *Kingdom of Heaven*. He read the script while on an airplane after completing his work in *Troy*, and saw that the movie would give him the chance to play a true hero. Unlike the wishy-washy Paris, the lead character in *Kingdom of Heaven*, named Balian, would be

Bloom worked again with director Ridley Scott in Kingdom of Heaven. *The two are shown here on the movie's set.*

sure of his convictions. The movie would also give him a chance to work once again with director Ridley Scott, who had won an Oscar for *Gladiator* since Bloom last worked with him on *Black Hawk Down*.

Bloom was not offered the role without an audition, however. He met with Scott for two hours to discuss the role, and after a few hours of sleep returned the next day to put on a beard and armor, learn several scenes from the movie, and do a screen test on camera. Two months later he learned he had won the part, and was soon on his way to film the movie in Spain and Morocco.

Kingdom of Heaven is set in Jerusalem during the twelfth century, during a lull between the Second and Third Crusades. Bloom once again begins the film as a blacksmith, the same occupation his character has in *Pirates*. Balian's wife and child die, and he struggles to understand why God would allow such tragedy in his life. Encouraged by his father, played by Liam Neeson, he becomes a knight in order to defend the city of Jerusalem. The role of Balian is also a romantic one, as the character becomes infatuated with a princess, played by Eva Green.

Extra Pressure

While the movie gave Bloom the opportunity to combine both his romantic and swashbuckling sides, it also placed additional pressure on him. This was Bloom's first leading role in a major picture. He had been afraid of failure when he was initially offered the role, unsure of whether he was ready to tackle a big role in such an expensive picture. However, while the fearful side of him made him wonder if he wanted to take it on, another side of him said he would be foolish not to. Always up for a challenge, Bloom accepted the opportunity to test his talent.

Bloom had watched carefully how Mortensen in *The Lord of the Rings*, Depp in *Pirates*, and Pitt in *Troy* had conducted themselves on the sets of their major films. He took note of how they prepared for the roles and how they thoughtfully brought their characters to life. Knowing that they had been able to accomplish what they had set out to do with their characters helped Bloom handle the pressure put on his shoulders for *Kingdom of Heaven*.

In addition to being mentally prepared, Bloom also wanted to be physically ready for the role. He put on about twenty pounds, eating as many as six meals a day and lifting weights to give himself a more impressive on-screen presence. In this picture, Bloom played a character growing from a boy into a man, and he saw the film as a coming-of-age movie for himself as well as his character.

Attracting Attention

With *Kingdom of Heaven*, Bloom got his wish of portraying a heroic character noted for his integrity. As the star of the movie, he attracted a great deal of attention when shooting began. When the actor arrived in Spain to make the picture, he found that young girls' infatuation with him had risen to a new level. There were thousands of girls shouting and crying when he appeared, and he had a hard time believing it was all because of him. In addition, the paparazzi followed him much more aggressively in Spain than they did in his native Britain.

The increased attention made it difficult for him to go about his day-to-day life. It was the first time he had been the object of that much attention; it took him by surprise. Bloom humbly accepted the adoration, but had been unprepared for the amount he would receive. He surmised that the large number of

Outstanding Bill

When Orlando Bloom treated his off-again, on-again girlfriend Kate Bosworth and a large group of friends to an elaborate party in honor of her birthday, he forgot about one thing: the bill. The group celebrated at the Casara Amarelo restaurant in Brazil, and when it came time to pay, Bloom tried to charge the $700-plus tab. However, the restaurant's credit card machine was broken that evening and the star could not settle up.

He took down the restaurant's address and promised to pay. However, several months later the restaurant owner had not heard from him. Knowing how busy the actor was, she imagined it was just an oversight and was not upset with Bloom for not following up with a check. "It wasn't his fault," owner Fe Behling told the British newspaper *Mirror*. "He did his best to pay the bill at the time."

Liam Neeson and Bloom appear in a scene from Kingdom of Heaven. *Bloom's celebrity status skyrocketed during the movie's filming.*

people interested in him was due to his being the star of a major movie being filmed in town, and his presence had been anticipated by the media. He was relieved to find that he was much more protected while filming in Morocco, and he appreciated the opportunity to go out without being constantly bothered by fans and photographers.

Bloom had come to accept the fact that he was considered a heartthrob by teenage girls. However, he tried not to let their admiration go to his head. Dominic Monaghan, who had acted beside Bloom in *Rings*, said he did not think his friend saw himself as a sex symbol. However, if it would help him get roles in good movies, he would not give up the title. Another friend told him that there would always be someone in the public eye whom girls dreamed of, and he recognized this status without becoming egotistical about it. "If that's where you find yourself, that's where you find yourself," he said. "If teenage girls relate to me as that, I guess I'm a lucky boy."[48]

The Next Level

Bloom was acknowledged as a popular young actor, but *Kingdom of Heaven* would test whether he could take that popularity up a notch. He had the lead in *Kingdom of Heaven*, and the movie would show whether he could attract large audiences to a picture in the way that more established stars like Pitt or Crowe could. Bloom had acted in major productions before, but had never had the central role. *Kingdom of Heaven* would be Bloom's opportunity to show that he could hold his own on-screen for the entire movie.

While he was grateful for the opportunity to star in such a major production, Bloom realized that he would have limited control over the final product. The movie was more director Scott's project than his. "When you're collaborating with Ridley Scott, it's his baby," Bloom says. "I feel like his is the top name on the slot."[49]

When the movie was released in May 2005, Bloom received some praise for the new maturity he brought to the role, but he and Scott also received criticism for delivering a product that failed to live up to expectations. Reviewer Richard Corliss spoke positively of Bloom's performance, saying "Bloom has matured splendidly (the beard helps). He gives Balian heft and winsomeness as a pensive man of action."[50] However, other reviewers did not think he brought enough strength to the role. "Unlike *Gladiator, Heaven* fails to tell a compelling tale and its protagonist is a milquetoast," wrote reviewer Leah Rozen in *People*. "The ambitious film's desert settings are sweeping, its costumes resplendent and Bloom gorgeous to gaze upon, but the whole adds up to a big yawn."[51]

Kingdom of Heaven topped the box office in its first weekend of release, pulling in $19.6 million. While more people went to see *Kingdom* than any other movie that weekend, its returns were still disappointing in relation to the cost of the film. Some questioned the choice of Bloom as the movie's lead actor. "He's still perceived as a pretty boy and hence not perceived as a manly man," says Brandon Gray, president of Box Office Mojo, which tracks the amount of money films bring in. "And that alienates the primary demographic for historical epics—adult males—more so than it attracts young females."[52] In addition, the movie was rated "R," which had the practical effect of preventing many young people from seeing it.

Elizabethtown

While Bloom did not always receive accolades when he tried new things, that did not prevent him from continuing to take on different types of roles. He did not want to alienate his young fan base, but he also wanted to expand his acting repertoire by making some movies that appealed to different types of audiences. In his next picture, he left historical dramas behind and accepted the male lead in a romantic film, *Elizabethtown*, with actress Kirsten Dunst. The movie also allowed him to pair up again with director Cameron Crowe, who had worked with Bloom on a Gap commercial shortly after the first *The Lord of the Rings* was released.

Elizabethtown offered Bloom the chance to show his quirky side, a lighter personality than he had presented in previous films. *Elizabethtown* is more of a love story than his other movies have been, as Bloom plays an American shoe designer who is devastated after he causes the Oregon company he works for to lose millions of dollars. He considers suicide, but is reminded how much he is needed after his father dies and he takes on the job of fulfilling his father's last wishes. On the flight back to his home in Kentucky he meets a flight attendant, played by Dunst, and begins a romance that helps him turn his life around.

The character-driven romantic film, with both dramatic and lighthearted moments, was very different from the heavy costumes, historical settings, and Bloom's action in previous major movies. It was the relationship between the two main characters that moved the story forward, although this time there were no swords or battles to hold the audience's attention. The actors' emotions and conversations would carry the scenes. Bloom again had the lead in the movie, and was taking on another challenge.

Timely Drama

When *Kingdom of Heaven* was released in May 2005, there was concern that the Christian-Muslim conflict in the film would be too close to real-life conflict in the Iraq War. However, director Ridley Scott said his intent with the movie was to show the importance of balancing idealism with humanitarianism. Rather than placing blame, it focuses on the time during the twelfth century when the Muslims and Christians fought over Jerusalem, in battles led by the Christian knight Balian of Ibelin and the great Muslim warrior Saladin.

Bloom explained that his character exemplifies the knight's code of being brave and truthful, and safeguarding the helpless. The conflict examined in the film has been going on for centuries, he noted. "People have been fighting over religion, over land, over water, over oil, over power," he said in an interview with Michele Hatty in *USA Weekend*. "It's been going on for hundreds of years, and it's not changing."

This movie was a love story, and he and Dunst were the film's main attractions.

A Movie Star with Heart

Bloom again showed his kindhearted side while making the movie. He became friends with Dunst while on the movie set, and comforted her when her relationship with her boyfriend ended. However, his actions sparked rumors that Bloom's girlfriend, Bosworth, was jealous of the attention he was paying to Dunst.

Bloom emphasized that he was just being a good friend by supporting Dunst when she was down. By October 2004, newspapers were reporting that Bosworth and Bloom had reconciled, and some reports said they were engaged. However, both denied the rumors.

Bosworth had been as reluctant as Bloom to reveal any details of their relationship. They both had homes in Los Angeles, but Bosworth stayed with Bloom when she was in London. In early 2004 Bloom had said publicly that he was in love with being in love, and enjoyed loving someone so much that he could not stop thinking about her. He visited Bosworth while she was making the movie, *Win a Date with Tad Hamilton!*, and those working on the set noticed Bloom and Bosworth exchanging loving glances. When Bosworth's movie *Beyond the Sea* premiered in December 2004, Bloom accompanied her to the screening and complimented her acting ability.

Bloom was not linked with any other women while he was with Bosworth, leading people to speculate that an engagement was imminent. He continued to romance her in January 2005 when he threw her a party at a restaurant in Brazil in honor of her twenty-second birthday. He invited their close friends to meet them there, and during the five-hour party they ate a lavish meal and Bloom hired a local band to sing "Happy Birthday" to his girlfriend.

A Pirate Once Again

Although Bloom and Bosworth enjoyed themselves that evening, time spent together was rare as their busy work schedules made it difficult for them to see each other as often as they would have liked. Bosworth was a busy actress, and Bloom did not let his career get sidetracked by personal issues. He continued to keep a hectic schedule, and in summer 2005 began making a sequel to *Pirates of the Caribbean*.

The movie was a safe bet for a hit and another chance for him to work with Depp. Although Bloom had proven that he was not afraid to stretch himself as an actor, he saw no problem with returning to a comfortable role when he had the chance. He would be making a pair of sequels at the same time, and saw the opportunity to add more depth to the character of Will Turner. In the sequels, Turner becomes more of a pirate, and struggles to come to grips with the motives behind his transformation from ordinary citizen to a swashbuckler on the high seas.

Happy Wanderer

Bloom's successful career was moving along at a steady clip, but it was at the expense of his relationship with Bosworth. In February 2005 they announced that they had ended their relationship. They briefly reconciled that spring and continued to see each other when they could, but later explained that they

In February 2005 Bloom ended his relationship with actress Kate Bosworth in order to focus on his career.

Bloom greets his fans at the premiere of Troy *in Cannes. Despite his many accomplishments in his short career, Bloom continues to grow as an actor.*

were both simply too busy with their careers to have a serious relationship. Bosworth hinted that when Bloom committed to making the *Pirates* sequels in summer 2005 rather than setting aside time to get married, she had had enough.

Bloom had been making movies in New Zealand, Australia, Malta, and Spain, and Bosworth would have been happy to have him settle down and spend some time with her. However, Bloom could not make that commitment. When the offer came to make the sequels to *Pirates of the Caribbean*, he could not pass it up. Bosworth also decided to make a career move, and took the part of Lois Lane in *Superman Returns*.

Looking for New Challenges

In 2005 Bloom was not ready to put his personal life above his blossoming career. The acting jobs he was being offered required a great deal of travel to set locations around the world and being away from home for long periods of time.

Bloom enjoys the challenges that come with each new role. He is constantly looking for new ways to stretch his skills as an actor, while learning to deal with the demands his fame and hectic schedule place upon his personal life. As busy as his schedule is, he does not intend to slow down just yet. Rather, he focuses on taking advantage of all the adventures his career has to offer.

Bloom is still in the first chapter of his career, and it amazes him to think about all he has already accomplished. He is thankful for the many opportunities he has had to work with and learn from well-known directors and stars, and he looks forward to continuing to learn and further his career. "Ultimately, I'm counting my lucky stars," he said, "but I know that there's a long way to go and there's a lot for me to do."[53]

Notes

Chapter 1: Untamed Enthusiasm

1. Quoted in Kevin Hillstrom, ed., "Orlando Bloom," *Biography Today*. Detroit: Omnigraphics, 2004, p. 23.
2. Quoted in BBC News, "Pirates Star's Early Promise." http://news.bbc.co.uk/go/pr/fr/1/hi/england/kent/3136767. stm.
3. Quoted in Nancy Mills, "The Ordeals of Orlando," *New York Daily News*, May 1, 2005. www.nydailynews.com/entertain ment/v-pfriendly/story/304920p-260910c.html.
4. Quoted in Hillstrom, *Biography Today*, p. 22.
5. Quoted in Rhonda Richford, "We Love Orlando!" *Teen People*, February 1, 2004, p. 78.
6. Quoted in *People*, "Greater Orlando," January 12, 2004, p. 26.
7. Quoted in Hillstrom, *Biography Today*, p. 23.
8. Quoted in Allison Glock, "Orlando's Magic," *GQ*, January 2004, p. 54.
9. Quoted in BBC News, "Pirates Star's Early Promise."

Chapter 2: Life-Changing Experience

10. Quoted in Ali Gazan and Martine Bury, "The Incredibly Charming Mr. Bloom," *YM*, January 2003, p. 61.
11. Quoted in Hillstrom, *Biography Today*, p. 24.
12. Quoted in "Orlando Bloom," *Biography Resource Center Online*, Gale Group, 2003. Reproduced in *Biography Resource Center*. Farmington Hills, MI: Thomson Gale, 2005.

13. Quoted in Glock, "Orlando's Magic," p. 54.

14. Quoted in Pippa Smith, *Orlando Bloom: Hollywood's New Heartthrob*, December 24, 2003. http://entertainment.iwon.com/celebgossip/star/id/12_24_2003.html.

15. Quoted in Glock, "Orlando's Magic," p. 54.

16. Quoted in Gazen and Bury, "The Incredibly Charming Mr. Bloom," p. 61.

17. Quoted in Brian Sibley, *The Lord of the Rings Official Movie Guide*, New York: Houghton Mifflin, 2001, p. 44.

Chapter 3: An Awesome Elf

18. Quoted in Hillstrom, *Biography Today*, p. 26.

19. Quoted in Hillstrom, *Biography Today*, p. 27.

20. Quoted in Mandi Bierly et al., "Orlando Bloom: (LEGO-LAS)," *Entertainment Weekly*, May 17, 2004, p. 16.

21. Quoted in Nick Webster, "Orlando Bloom on Life as a Sex Symbol," Mirror.co.uk. www.mirror.co.uk_printable.version.cfm?mthod=printable_version_mirror&obhectid=.

22. Quoted in Gazen and Bury, "The Incredibly Charming Mr. Bloom," p. 60.

23. Quoted in Gillian Flynn, "The Making of an Epic," *Entertainment Weekly*, May 17, 2004, p. 28.

24. Quoted in Hillstrom, *Biography Today*, p. 30.

Chapter 4: Hero and Heartthrob

25. Quoted in Henry Cabot Beck, "Orlando Bloom," *Interview*, November 2001, p. 50.

26. Lisa Schwarzbaum, "Force of Hobbits," *Entertainment Weekly*, December 14, 2001, p. 50.

27. Quoted in David Keeps et al., "The 25 Hottest Stars Under 25," *Teen People*, June 1, 2002, p. 99.

28. Quoted in Glock, "Orlando's Magic," p. 54.

29. Quoted in Hillstrom, *Biography Today*, p. 35.

30. Quoted in Hillstrom, *Biography Today*, p. 35.

31. Quoted in Kate Stroup, "Orlando Bloom: The Budding of a Heartthrob," *Newsweek*, July 14, 2003, p. 56.

32. Lisa Schwarzbaum, "Ned Kelly: Outback Outlaws Outwit,

Outplay, and Outlast the Odds," *Entertainment Weekly*, April 2, 2004, p. 45.

33. Quoted in Hillstrom, *Biography Today*, p. 32.

Chapter 5: Working with the Best

34. Quoted in Jeff Chu, "A British Star in Full Bloom," *Time International*, August 11, 2003, p. 52.

35. Quoted in Hillstrom, *Biography Today*, p. 30.

36. Quoted in Hillstrom, *Biography Today*, p. 30.

37. Quoted in Susan Wloszczyna, "Orlando Watches Fame Bloom on the High Seas," *USA Today*, June 7, 2003. www.usatoday.com/life/movies/news/2003-07-06-orlando_x.htm.

38. Quoted in Allison Adato, "Bachelor No. 1," *People Weekly*, June 28, 2004, p. 66.

39. Richard Corliss, "A Rollickingly Entertaining Ride," *Time*, July 4, 2003, p. 61.

40. Quoted in Gillian Flynn, "Men and Myth," *Entertainment Weekly*, May 14, 2004, p. 24.

41. Quoted in Flynn, "Men and Myth," p. 24.

42. Quoted in Chu, "A British Star in Full Bloom," p. 52.

Chapter 6: Orlando Blooms

43. Leah Rozen, "Troy: Brad Pitt, Eric Bana, Orlando Bloom, Peter O'Toole, Julie Christie, Diane Kruger, Brian Cox, Sean Bean," *People Weekly*, May 24, 2004, p. 29.

44. Rozen, "Troy: Brad Pitt, Eric Bana, Orlando Bloom, Peter O'Toole, Julie Christi, Diane Kruger, Brian Cox, Sean Bean," p. 29.

45. Todd McCarthy, "'Troy' Toys with Greek Epic," *Variety*, May 10, 2004, p. 46.

46. Quoted in Hillstrom, *Biography Today*, p. 34.

47. Eddie Cockrell, "Haven," *Variety*, September 27, 2004, p. 81.

48. Quoted in Fred Topel, "Baby Bloom," *The Wave Magazine*. www.thewavemag.com/printarticle.php?articleid=25276.

49. Quoted in Adam Kane, "Orlando Bloom Talks about James Bond and *Kingdom of Heaven*," Wizard News. www.wizardnews.com/story/20050408.html.

50. Richard Corliss, "To War or Not to War," *Time*, May 9, 2005, p. 65.

51. Leah Rozen, "Kingdom of Heaven: Orlando Bloom, Liam Neeson, Jeremy Irons, Eva Green," *People Weekly*, May 16, 2005, p. 40.

52. Quoted in John Lippman and Amir Efrati, "'Heaven' Can Wait," *The Wall Street Journal*, May 13, 2005, p. W3.

53. Quoted in Becca Shader, "Flix: Orlando Bloom Interview," *Co-Ed Magazine*. www.co-edmagazine.com/article/cfm?articleid=342.

Important Dates in the Life of Orlando Bloom

January 13, 1977
Orlando Bloom is born in Canterbury, England.

1993
Orlando leaves Canterbury to study acting at Britain's National Youth Theatre.

1994
Orlando gets his first acting job, a one-time appearance on the British television drama series *Casualty*.

1995
After spending two seasons with the youth theater, Orlando continues his acting education at the British American Drama Academy.

1997
Orlando makes his first on-screen appearance in *Wilde*, but puts a professional acting career on hold to attend the Guildhall School of Music and Drama in London.

1998
A three-story fall almost paralyzes Bloom, and he spends nearly a year recovering from his accident.

1999
A few days before graduating from Guildhall, Bloom is selected to play Legolas in *The Lord of the Rings* trilogy. Before he leaves

England to make the movies in New Zealand, he also films a small role in the British television drama *Midsomer Murders*.

2001
The Lord of the Rings: The Fellowship of the Ring is released, and Bloom quickly becomes a heartthrob for teenage girls. He also has a small role in *Black Hawk Down*.

2002
Bloom again appears on-screen as Legolas in *The Lord of the Rings: The Two Towers*. He makes *Ned Kelly* in Australia and *The Calcium Kid* in Britain, both released in the United States in 2004.

2003
The final installment in the *Rings* series, *The Lord of the Rings: The Return of the King*, is released. Bloom also makes his first appearance as blacksmith-turned-pirate Will Turner in *Pirates of the Caribbean*.

2004
Bloom plays Paris in the Trojan War epic *Troy*, and moves away from historical films with a role in the low-budget *Haven*.

2005
Bloom makes his first appearance as a leading man in *Kingdom of Heaven*. He also stars in *Elizabethtown*, his first major movie that is not a costume drama, and begins filming two sequels to *Pirates of the Caribbean*.

For Further Reading

Books

Heather Kranenburg, *Lovin' Bloom*. New York: Random House, 2004. This paperback looks at Bloom's life and favorite things.

A.C. Parfitt, *Orlando Bloom: The Biography*. London: John Blake, 2004. This stylish account of Orlando's life includes photos of his hometown and background on his parents.

Robert Steele, *Orlando Bloom*. London: Plexus, 2004. This glossy book details the early part of Bloom's career, with many pictures and quotes from his interviews.

Web Sites

Full Bloom–All Orlando, All The Time (www.full-bloom. net). This site offers news about Bloom from throughout the world, as well as notices of television appearances. It also includes a great archive of Bloom-related articles.

Official Orlando Bloom Web Site (www.theofficialorlando bloomsite.com). Hear Bloom speak, and read his answers to fans' questions on his official Web site.

Orlando Bloom Files (www.theobfiles.com). This fan site has plenty of articles and up-to-date news about Bloom.

Works Consulted

Books

Kevin Hillstrom, ed., "Orlando Bloom," *Biography Today*. Detroit: Omnigraphics, 2004. A brief look at Bloom's early career.

Brian Sibley, *The Lord of the Rings Official Movie Guide*. New York: Houghton Mifflin, 2001. A picture-heavy glimpse at the movie's actors.

Periodicals

Allison Adato, "Bachelor No. 1," *People Weekly*, June 28, 2004.

Mandi Bierly et al, "Orlando Bloom: (LEGOLAS)," *Entertainment Weekly*, May 17, 2004.

Anthony Breznican, "Epics Struggle," *USA Today*, April 20, 2005.

Henry Cabot Beck, "Orlando Bloom," *Interview*, November 2001.

Jennifer Calonita-Smith, "What's New," *Teen People*, February 1, 2002.

Jeff Chu, "A British Star in Full Bloom," *Time International*, August 11, 2003.

Eddie Cockrell, "Haven," *Variety*, September 27, 2004.

Richard Corliss, "A Rollickingly Entertaining Ride," *Time*, July 4, 2003.

———, "To War or Not to War," *Time*, May 9, 2005.

Tom Cunneff, "And You Are?" *People Weekly*, January 19, 2004.

Entertainment Weekly, "IT Elf—Orlando Bloom," June 27/July 4, 2003.

Gillian Flynn, "The Making of an Epic," *Entertainment Weekly*, May 17, 2004.

———, "Men and Myth," *Entertainment Weekly*, May 14, 2004.

Ali Gazan and Martine Bury, "The Incredibly Charming Mr. Bloom," *YM*, January 2003.

Allison Glock, "Orlando's Magic," *GQ*, January 2004.

Michele Hatty, "It's His Time to Bloom," *USA Weekend*, April 29–May 1, 2005.

David Keeps et al., "The 25 Hottest Stars Under 25," *Teen People*, June 1, 2002.

Knight-Ridder/Tribune News Service, "Bloom Gets Medieval in 'Kingdom,'" October 29, 2003.

———, "Bloom is Britain's Sexiest Actor," June 17, 2004.

———, "Bloom's Career Continues to Blossom," November 6, 2003.

———, "Bloom Tops 'Hottest Bachelor' list," June 21, 2004.

———, "'Lord of the Rings' Elf Encourages Reading," October 20, 2003.

John Lippman and Amir Efrati, "'Heaven' Can Wait," *Wall Street Journal*, May 13, 2005.

Jason Lynch, Carrie Bell, and Sara Hammel, "Oh, What a Knight!" *People Weekly*, May 16, 2005.

Todd McCarthy, "'Troy' Toys with Greek Epic," *Variety*, May 10, 2004.

People Weekly, "Greater Orlando," January 12, 2004.

———, "Orlando Bloom & Kate Bosworth," February 14, 2005.

Rhonda Richford, "We Love Orlando!" *Teen People*, February 1, 2004.

Leah Rozen, "Kingdom of Heaven: Orlando Bloom, Liam Neeson, Jeremy Irons, Eva Green," *People Weekly*, May 16, 2005.

———, "Troy: Brad Pitt, Eric Bana, Orlando Bloom, Peter O'-Toole, Julie Christie, Diane Kruger, Brian Cox, Sean Bean," *People Weekly*, May 24, 2004.

Lisa Schwarzbaum, "Force of Hobbits," *Entertainment Weekly*, December 14, 2001.

———, "Ned Kelly: Outback Outlaws Outwit, Outplay, and Outlast the Odds," *Entertainment Weekly*, April 2, 2004.

————, "Ship of Ghouls," *Entertainment Weekly*, July 18, 2003.

Kate Stroup, "OHMIGOD! A Heartthrob in Bloom," *Newsweek*, June 17, 2002.

————, "Orlando Bloom: The Budding of a Heartthrob," *Newsweek*, July 14, 2003.

Teen People, "Full Bloom," December 1, 2002.

UPI NewsTrack, "Bloom Worked out for 'Troy' Role," May 17, 2004.

Vanity Fair, "The Heartthrob; Orlando Bloom, Actor," March 2004.

Chris William, "Ned Kelly," *Entertainment Weekly*, August 6, 2004.

Internet Sources

BBC News, "Pirates Star's Early Promise." http://news.bbc.co.uk/go/pr/fr/1/hi/england/kent/3136767.stm.

Ian Caddell, "Orlando Blooms." www.straight.com/content/cfm?id=9812.

Contactmusic.com, "Love on Hold for Bloom and Bosworth." www.contactmusic.com/new/xmlfeed.nsf/mdnwebpages/love%20on%20hold%20for%20bloom%20and%20bosworth.

Female First Womens Lifestyle Magazine, "Kate Bosworth Reveals Why She and Orlando Bloom Split." www.femalefirst.co.uk/celebrity/24152004.htm.

Lee-Ann Fullerton and Beverley Lyons, "The Razz: Knightly Blossoms for Bloom." www.dailyrecord.co.uk/printable_version.cfm?objectid=13788719&siteid=89488.

Adam Kane, "Orlando Bloom Talks About James Bond and *Kingdom of Heaven*," Wizard News. www.wizardnews.com/story/20050408.html.

Nancy Mills, "The Ordeals of Orlando," *New York Daily News*, May 1, 2005. www.nydailynews.com/entertainment/v-p friendly/story/304920p-260910c.html.

Mirror, "Orlando's Big Bloomer." www.mirror.co.uk/printable_version.cfm?objectid=15452240&siteid=94762.

"Orlando Bloom," *Biography Resource Center Online*, Gale Group, 2003. Reproduced in *Biography Resource Center*. Farmington Hills, MI: Thomson Gale, 2005.

Daniel Saney, "Orlando Adjusts to Fame." www.digitalspy.co.uk /article/ds20765.html.

Becca Shader, "Flix: Orlando Bloom Interview," *Co-Ed Magazine*. www.co-edmagazine.com/article/cfm?articleid=342.

Pippa Smith, Orlando Bloom: Hollywood's New Heartthrob, *Star*, http://web.starmagazine.com/news/60216.

Fred Topel, "Baby Bloom," *The Wave Magazine*. www.thewave mag.com/printarticle.php?articleid=25276.

Nick Webster, "Orlando Bloom on Life as a Sex Symbol," Mirror.co.uk. www.mirror.co.uk_printable.version.cfm?mthod= printable_version_mirror&obhectid=.

Susan Wloszczyna, "Orlando Watches Fame Bloom on the High Seas," *USA Today*, June 7, 2003. www.usatoday.com/life/ movies/news/2003-07-06-orlando_x.htm.

Index

Picture Credits

About the Author

Terri Dougherty enjoys writing books for children and has written biographies on Mary-Kate and Ashley Olsen, Julia Roberts, Tim Allen, and Brad Pitt, among others. Terri was a newspaper reporter and editor before beginning her freelance writing career and still writes magazine and newspaper articles. Terri grew up in Black Creek, Wisconsin, and now lives in Appleton, Wisconsin, with her husband, Denis, and their three children, Kyle, Rachel, and Emily. When she has the time, she likes watching *The Lord of the Rings* movies with her son.